'[Written with] passion, erudition, and fluidity ... Provocative and always willing to take on the conventional wisdom, Nyabola emerges with this book as an important observer.'

'A valiant exploration of one of humanity's most fundamental needs: the freedom to move. Drawing on a captivating life of her own, Nanjala Nyabola powerfully reminds us of the complexity of human identity. Above all, an incredibly moving book.'

David Lammy MP, author of *Tribes: How Our Need to Belong Can Make or Break Society*

'Nyabola's insightful essays deal with identity and the notion of home and belonging, in a world challenged by mobility and dislocation. This collection joins a venerable tradition of Black essay-writing, as it discovers for the socially aware traveller new routes and philosophies to explore.'

Margaret Busby, editor of *New Daughters of Africa*

'In the great tradition of Said, Orwell and Bessie Head, Nyabola's is a profound, gripping and beautiful book of undeniable genius on exile, migration and travel in our catastrophic times. It speaks to all those committed to truth and justice.'

Cornel West, author of *Race Matters* and Professor of the Public Practice of Philosophy, Harvard University

'What a book! Nyabola takes us on a travel odyssey and an inner quest, and with her we recognise what remains undone and how we see or unsee others. Lethal and restless, yet tender and vulnerable. Disturbing, delicious, defiant. A triumph.'

Yvonne Adhiambo Owuor, author of *Dust and The Dragonfly Sea*

'A unique, provocative and thoughtful collection of essays. Part autobiography and travelogue, but also a powerful reflection on migration, travel, identity, racism, literature, language, Pan-Africanism and the experiences of a young Kenyan woman travelling throughout the modern world.'

Hakim Adi, Professor of the History of Africa and the African Diaspora, University of Chichester, and author of *Pan-Africanism: A History*

'At a time where the freedom of Black people to exist and move safely feels compromised, Nyabola's collection of essays on travelling is an urgent intervention which powerfully marries cultural and political exploration to the intricacies of modern Black identity.'

Jaso

T0003335

NANJALA NYABOLA

Travelling While Black

Essays Inspired by a Life on the Move

HURST & COMPANY, LONDON

First published in the United Kingdom in 2020 by
C. Hurst & Co. (Publishers) Ltd.,
41 Great Russell Street, London, WC1B 3PL
Copyright © Nanjala Nyabola, 2020
All rights reserved.
Printed in the United Kingdom by Bell & Bain Ltd, Glasgow.

The right of Nanjala Nyabola to be identified as the author
of this publication is asserted by her in accordance with the
Copyright, Designs and Patents Act, 1988.

A Cataloguing-in-Publication data record for this book
is available from the British Library.

ISBN: 9781787383821

A version of Chapter 2 was published by *On She Goes* as "What Travel Has Taught Me about Fear" (2017). A version of Chapter 3 was published by *Foreign Affairs* as "Strange Fruit" (2015). A version of Chapter 4 was published by *Foreign Affairs* in 2019. Chapter 7 is based on "Failed decolonisation of South African cities fuels violence" (2019), published by *Al Jazeera English*, and "The African is Not at Home" (2015), published by *The New Inquiry*. A version of Chapter 13 was published by *Al Jazeera English* as "The politics of identity and belonging in Kenya" (2014). A version of Chapter 16 was published by *On She Goes* in 2017.

This book is printed using paper from registered sustainable and managed sources.

www.hurstpublishers.com

CONTENTS

Acknowledgements   ix
Foreword   xi

1. *M'Pa Blan*: I Am Not White   1
2. Travelling While Black   31
3. A Thousand Words   39
4. The End of Asylum   53
5. The Sea That Eats Our Children   61
6. Looking For Bessie   87
7. The African Is Not at Home   115
8. Periodic Offerings to the Visa Gods   135
9. Africa For Beginners   143
10. *Ukabila*   149
11. This Is For the Community   161
12. Small Acts of Resistance   175
13. Who Do You Say I Am?   185
14. Sagarmatha   193
15. *Tero Buru* of Collective Grief   201
16. Oh, The Places You'll Pee!   217
17. On Race   221

Further Reading   237

ACKNOWLEDGEMENTS

Writing is always a process of collective action even if only one name appears on the cover. This book was born through a moment of tremendous flux and adjustment for the world and myself, at a time when there was no institutional support to make this work. Special thanks to Aaron Bady, Ty McCormick, Mariya Petkova and all the amazing editors I have had the privilege of working with throughout my career, who reviewed and commented on earlier versions of some of these essays. Sincere thanks also to the entire team at Hurst, including Michael Dwyer and Lara Weisweiller-Wu for their patience while working through very uncertain times. Thank you to all the friends whose conversation gave much needed perspective in uncertain times. And finally to my family—for their patience, and for finally coming around to the idea of writing as a profession.

FOREWORD

This is not a travel memoir.

One month after I finished the first draft of this essay collection, many of the assumptions about how the world works—particularly in the context of travel—were challenged by the arrival of an aggressive flu-like virus called COVID-19. Because the outbreak began in China, many racist assumptions about Chinese diets and lifestyles have been rehashed around the world since the start of 2020. People were quick to ostracise Chinese and East Asian individuals and eateries, and there were a spate of verbal and physical attacks on people of Asian descent across Europe and North America—on buses, in the street, online. Even the US president and his ambassadors invited people to call COVID-19 "the Wuhan virus" or "the Chinese Flu".

However, the disease quickly moved to Europe and took root there, killing thousands within a matter of weeks, and suddenly the realities of privilege and race in travel were laid bare. Countries scrambled to close their borders as an emergency measure, but in a world built for the free circulation of wealthy people, the idea of locking a disease into a single geography proved hollow. The coronavirus galloped through rich nations and forced poorer ones to examine some of the presumptions that dictate who gets to travel freely. After decades of shoring up

Fortress Europe against imagined threats of invasion from Africa and Asia, suddenly it was African and Asian countries imposing travel bans on Europeans.

Yet some habits proved harder to break than others. By March 2020, even though Africa was the part of the world least affected at the time, the spectre of anti-black racism had reared its head. It didn't matter that reality had completely reversed the popular-culture narrative of mysterious, quick-killing diseases emerging from the Heart of Darkness and spreading across the world. It didn't matter that the dreaded virus had come to Africa, rather than from it. Black and African people quickly became the target for unspoken fears of contagion, even if the death and destruction in both East and West had been caused by the political choices of leaders in those regions. Somehow, black people were expected to carry the cost.

In China, landlords summarily evicted African tenants while local stores banned Africans from entering. In the US and the UK, hospitals turned away black people presenting with symptoms of the disease only to have them die later at home—a recurring problem of disbelieving black pain when it is presented in hospitals. Travel from African countries was banned long before rich countries shut down travel from fellow wealthy nations. On the high seas of the Mediterranean and in camps near borders, European countries used the disease as a pretext for refusing to admit refugees. This pandemic, grafted onto centuries of bias and exclusion, has contributed to a disproportionate impact of the disease on non-white populations everywhere, ravaging already-disenfranchised communities.

This is a cost that black and brown people often bear. In the modern age, we live under disproportionately harsh policing of our movements even within our own communities. Beyond lockdowns and quarantines, we have always known what it means for our movements to be unfree. Uprooting, dislocation and restriction reach deep into the places we call home, particularly when our societies become the terrain for other people's wars. It's difficult to think of these things as abstract objects of fascination when your body is one of the millions onto which the violence of racism is projected daily. Even as the coronavirus has brought a real prospect of permanent changes to the way we travel, for those of us accustomed to the rough edges of human mobility, our concern is that the system will simply find new ways of pathologising our movements.

This fear—and the sudden stark obviousness with which we've seen the life-and-death stakes of a racist world since COVID began—have moved us to action: 2020 was the year that hundreds of thousands—perhaps even millions—of people around the world braved a pandemic to remind their political leaders that, despite centuries of state-sanctioned violence, institutional racism and exclusion, black lives do in fact matter. The protests have forced a reckoning in the global conversation around race. In this book, I try to expand and deepen this reckoning through some uncomfortable stories of being on the move.

I am not an expert in the study of race. I am a traveller. I travel a lot, for work and for myself; and I spent many years studying human mobility. I experienced first-hand the disconnect of entering societies as an ethnic and economic minority, but also witnessed, documented and advocated against other people's experiences of displacement. I was operating in a professional environment where race and racism—in the unspoken tenets of white saviourism—were embedded in the very logic of the organisations doing this work, but could never be uttered out loud. This is reflected in guidebooks, which offer subjective notions of which societies are the most dangerous and which are the most accessible, yet never spare a word for how race factors into the equation. Human mobility can strip both visitor and host society of many of the superfluous bells and whistles that normally keep us in denial about how kind, hospitable or just we are.

When I first started backpacking, I had a long list of requirements that needed to be met before I could even consider going somewhere. Today I more or less have three—and even that is more than most people on the move can afford to allow themselves. Today, I only ask for a clean and safe hotel. An easy visa process. And a means to get there and back. This list has been whittled down over years of travel in almost seventy countries, after finding myself in situations that I would never previously have contemplated. Sleeping on an airport floor in Madrid when your hotel locks you out. Running for the Ghanaian border when your Togolese employer turns out to be abusive. Running out of money in Burkina Faso and having to depend on the kindness of strangers. Battling altitude sickness on the slopes of Mount Everest. Once you've found yourself in a situation where you had to depend on a foreign society's hospitality to survive, your list of non-negotiables changes very quickly.

Mobility rubs away at so many of the things that we think are necessary for life. When we move not out of choice, but out of necessity, we encounter other societies at their best or at their worst. Gasping for air in a foreign language at the side of a mountain leaves you thinking about what actually matters in life. Having an influx of people from disparate backgrounds show up at your border reveals the truth about the societies we live in. Are the promises of equality and inclusion real, or are they things we tell ourselves to cope with the nasty and brutish circumstances of our lives? How do we process hospitality across difference—do we expect people to change and to become who we are, or do we make room for different expressions of kinship and fraternity? Do we allow people to determine their own identities, or do we expect them to be consumed by ours? Is it still empathy if we feel we have to know the individuals who arrive in our societies before we can be civil and welcoming? If we can only be kind to those who are on the move with a hefty measure of privilege?

* * *

Travel is not migration. Travel is merely a small dose of what is experienced by those who leave, knowing they can never go back. But it has given me a lot of time and opportunity to think about these things. I didn't leave Kenya for the first time until I was almost 20 years old. Up to that point, travel in my family meant visiting our grandparents in the village every year or two. We weren't even one of the families that go to Mombasa on holiday—that was a luxury beyond our imagination. I think this is partly why I became such an avid reader and writer: as a kid I had to imagine all of these experiences that I couldn't have in my real life, and everything I knew about the world was filtered through those newspapers and books I was reading so voraciously. Without travel, I simply would have gone on believing them.

Travel has forced my mind open in a way that books alone could not. I'm not oblivious to the fact that my ability to travel the way I do is predicated on a great deal of privilege. Beyond money, I am physically able to go to most places. I have had access to language education. I have a passport. (I also recognise that the world would be a much worse place if even 10 per cent more of the global population travelled as much as I do; it would be catastrophic for the environment.) My academic life has opened up the world to me in a way that it absolutely does not for other people of the same age and a similar background to mine. As we speak, millions of people around the world—most of them young and many of them in Africa—are on the move in search of some of the space and opportunity that life has afforded me. Many will die along the way. Some will lose everything. So I don't take for granted the fact that I can travel without those fears.

Still, seeing myself in the eyes of others has taught me a lot about the nature of race and gender, and other lines we draw in our societies. Something about a lone African woman travelling provokes interesting reactions in people. Shopkeepers watching me as I peruse the aisles in American and Western European pharmacies, and open hostility in Central Europe. Uninhibited curiosity in Asia, and complete indifference or comical enthusiasm in Africa. Being inappropriately propositioned by men who imagine that travelling solo is a declaration of sexual availability. I've learnt that simply by turning up, you force people to contend with their own preconceptions of what blackness and womanhood can be. To travel the way I do—often alone, with nothing more than a backpack and a vague itinerary—is to give yourself over completely to another society and its biases. It challenges you to either continue being fearless and turning up, or to walk away and return to your comfort zone. I've learnt to choose fearlessness.

Travel has systematically both enforced and undermined my belief in human nature. Race, age and gender are lenses through which other people see you and measure your ability to navigate a space. It's the difference between someone calling you a cab because "Accra is dangerous" or letting you walk the 10 metres because they think you can deal with it; it's the way people open doors for white men, but not for other people. Joe Shmoe may be able to backpack across Lomé with nothing more than the clothes on his back; you probably can't.

But I've also experienced the inverse. In Burkina Faso, I experienced so much hospitality I was embarrassed. I never once ate in a restaurant for the entire duration of my stay. Strangers welcomed me into their homes and overfed me because they'd never seen a Kenyan before. They were bowled over by my broken French. They couldn't wait to show me off to their friends. Lying beneath the stars in the Danakil region of Ethiopia, I had a profound conversation on the future of Africa as my young guide saw it. I had the same kind of welcome in Madagascar, and again in Egypt. My Africanness gave me an opening into the lives of my hosts that other travellers—white, Western or wealthy—may never be able to experience. And I learnt that the guidebook-writers conditioning people to be afraid of Africa might not be experiencing the same Africa as I am.

I brought a lot of these experiences into my professional life in refugee and displacement advocacy. I began to see the things that institutions would not name—the idea that a Western traveller overstaying their visa is harmless, but a black tourist doing the same is a criminal who must be met with the full force of the law. I saw the inequalities that shaped how differently I, an African, was treated in many parts of the world, even with all of my privilege; I watched it being formalised as procedure, intensified and forced onto people at their most vulnerable. But I also saw something that national narratives often obscure: the communities on the frontline of these debates—in Palermo, Johannesburg and in New York City—who are pushing back against their national leaders, and asking if a different way is possible. Travel gave me ideas that ran against the grain of dominant thought on managing human mobility, and I began to think that maybe I had an experience or a voice to bring to these international conversations that could otherwise be missing.

Many of the ideas I have about migration have been forged out of my work, but refined by my own life as a traveller. It is difficult to be abstract about hostile borders when you know what it feels to be pulled out of the immigration line and sent for "further screening" because you are the only black person in the group. It is difficult to theorise border walls when the people in flimsy boats undulating on the open water look like they could be your high school classmates, or your childhood neighbour. It is difficult to believe in the idea of one correct way of managing human movement when you know first-hand that there are so many exceptions to all the apparent rules; exceptions built on nothing more than a sense that the person seeking them is "one of us".

As you can imagine, these ideas have not gone over well with the academy, and so this book is something of a farewell letter to a professional space I have known well, but struggled to make sense of. The speed at which so many corners of the world have collapsed into racism and hate around the COVID-19 pandemic reminds us that racism is humanity's original sin—as crude violence, yes, but also as bureaucratic exclusion. And until the people claiming to help those who experience racism can bring themselves to name the beast, I don't see how the system can change. Migrants and refugees have been the canaries in the coal mine of a system that can no longer hold. This global outbreak has stripped so many of our societies of their safety nets. Illusions of modernity and of what remains can be encouraging—networks of mutual aid and community support—but also appalling—people who would waste their anxious breath on fomenting and disseminating hate. This is who we are when distilled to our anxieties, stripped of our pretensions of progress, and face-to-face with ourselves.

As a traveller, I feel a kinship and affinity with this struggle, which led me to advocacy and writing. My instinct when writing about complex things has been to retreat into academia, because it offers a sterile and agnostic environment that makes broad, sweeping claims possible—even desirable. But as a feminist scholar, I know that stories and personal narratives can do more than theory to communicate these insidious lines of fracture—the ones that only become visible to power, and people close to it, in moments of crisis. Those of us who collide regularly with the reality of racism are never really surprised by it. A government can tell itself that its immigration law is a neutral administrative enterprise, but those of us interacting with it and inhabiting the bodies this structure is designed to vilify and exclude—we know the truth. There is nothing neutral or even natural about the way these systems work. They are often designed to formalise and give a veneer of orthodoxy to power's unspoken hatreds and fears.

So this book sits somewhere between the philosophical and the personal. I don't think it's enough to just name the insidious racisms that shape the politics of human mobility: I think we have to stop and contemplate how they produce violence, and how that violence harms others. Sometimes theory doesn't go far enough to name these harms. That's why I've mostly been working as an independent consultant for the past decade: in my former workplaces, I met complex bureaucracies more focused on protecting the status quo, regardless of how much it was failing people, than on confronting widespread displacement and racism as real-life symptoms of a world on fire. We could never say that a policy was racist. We could never observe that our management hierarchies were organised by race. Here was this phenomenon having a tangible effect on everything that we did, but we were never allowed to name it, and therefore never in a position to deal with it.

So I want to tell uncomfortable stories, and then think about why they matter and why they make us uncomfortable. But I especially want to do this from a place that doesn't pretend that race can ever be abstract. In this book I want to sit in the discomfort of being a black woman and having our intersectional pain ignored. I want to record the unease of being a middle-class African watching my peers disembark on European shores after dangerous journeys fleeing the place I call home. I want to reflect on what it means to be at home, and to be un-homed. I want to lay bare the dissonance of Africans claiming Pan-Africanism while embracing xenophobia. I want to think a little bit about what racism looks like, both at the extremities of power dispar-ity, and also in those fuzzy middles that we are only just starting to square up to.

This is not a travel memoir. These are essays inspired by travel, about the way it changed what I think matters and about the ideas that come from dislocation. In *Reflections on Exile and Other Essays*, Edward Said wrote that the "image of traveler depends not on power, but on motion, on a willingness to go into different worlds, use different idioms, understand a variety of disguises, masks, rhetorics ... Travelers must suspend the claim of customary routine, in order to live in new rhythms and ritu-als." Travel in its broadest sense is about disrupted notions of home, and making room for difference within that. Mobility—itinerance, pastoralism, migration, travel, movement—changes the way we think about place and belonging, and this can be disorienting in a world where we are all expected to be fixed to one place. This is the tension I want to explore.

These essays are a vigil for all those people on the move who crash into a world that wants them to return. These essays come from moving through the world as a black, African woman, and from the opportunities and contradictions that creates. They are reflections on the joy, violence, hope, confusion, welcome and exclusion that people like me witness and endure, as we move through a world that has been moulded to exact harm on us. Human mobility contains so many categories of people—I have been a migrant, a tourist and an expat, never a refugee or dis-placed person, but spending much of my career working with both. Each of these experiences has set me on a journey to devel-oping a politics or a philosophy of human mobility. This book is a start in making that politics public.

These are reflections on dislocation, disjuncture, exile, alien-ation, belonging and their logical opposites. Some are essays about a broken world and the people who slip through its cracks.

FOREWORD

Some are about the limits of fixing our ideas of home to a single place. Some are about the walls we build to keep each other out. Some are about me, as an individual at the crossroads of all of this. Who are we when we are not at home? Or when the presumptions that we have about everyone belonging somewhere are taken away from us, either by force or by choice? What political practice emerges from that?

I don't think I have all the answers, but this is where I begin, hopefully: by asking the right questions.

Italy, 2020

1

M'PA BLAN

I AM NOT WHITE

I arrive in Haiti under the summer glare. It is hot—hotter than I imagined it would be, and possibly the hottest place that I've been thus far. It is the worst kind of heat, interwoven with a stifling humidity that envelopes you and presses against your nose and skin relentlessly. I am scared. Everything that I know about Haiti has been filtered through mainstream US media, and in the shadow of the recent earthquake, I am worried about chaos and upheaval. My mind spins as it tries to come up with a way to escape the weight of the air. I don't know if I'm ready to be here.

I will be in Port-au-Prince for some months, working as a community organiser and law clerk for a local human rights non-profit group. The idea is to provide some support for the organisation while also developing my own skills as a legal and community advocate—something in between a lawyer and an activist, which is where I've settled on what comes next for me. On the flight from New York City to Port-au-Prince, I am one of a handful of black faces on the plane and, to my knowledge, the only one not returning home after a long stay *lot bo*—"over there"—in the United States.

I am sitting next to a missionary from Indiana who tells me that this is the first time he's been on a plane. Not a plane to Haiti. A plane, ever. He doesn't know what to do with his customs and immigration forms—he's unsure how to answer some of the questions. For a few minutes I see him hesitate to reach out for help, before he finally concedes that I may be a more experienced traveller than he is, and he asks me. A vindictive elf on my shoulder smiles smugly: the American asking the African for help. Hundreds of years of history overturned in one interaction. I suppress my instinctive self-satisfied grin. A more rational elfin counterpart is alarmed—why is this man even here? What kind of person commits to Haiti as their first life adventure? Should Haiti be worried?

By this time, everything that I have read about Haiti has advised me to be afraid. My family warns me to be wary of voodoo, even though I have already survived a summer in Togo and Benin, birthplace of the religion they know there as *voudoun*. My childhood friends are worried that Haiti sounds dangerous. More so than our hometown Nairobi, which has the inglorious distinction of being one of the most dangerous cities in Africa. They warn me to be careful. Law school classmates think that I am being "brave" for choosing to spend a summer immersed in a new community instead of sifting through reams of legal jargon and paperwork as a summer associate. I don't feel particularly brave. I feel like choosing to spend ten weeks in Haiti is a much better decision than being holed up in a windowless office in Manhattan, doing document review for another billion-dollar corporation, mortgaging my long-term happiness at a job I already know I will hate. I hear many "whys", but I cannot offer a satisfying "because". I'm just going to Haiti, mostly because it's there.

M'PA BLAN: I AM NOT WHITE

I have tried to condense everything I will need for the next two and a half months of my life into a single suitcase. Normally, I would only take a backpack, but because I am travelling for work, I must pack many artefacts of the modern female existence. "Pack sanitary towels," someone tells me, "they don't really sell the good ones in Haiti." "You'll need a pair of heels. Haitian women dress up for work." "You'll never be able to find shampoo that works with your hair." Even though most people's hair in Haiti is presumably the same as mine? I don't wear heels in my regular life—it seems unwise to start now? And no good sanitary towels ... at all? When did being a woman get so complicated? What do men worry about when they pack for long trips away? Or do they just pick up their suitcases and go?

As soon as we land, I rush into the airport. Airports are my least favourite parts of travel. In Europe and North America, I am scrutinised intently—my dark skin held up against the bright surveillance lights, its secrets unpacked coarsely to determine if I am in fact a "good" immigrant, simply passing through or loaded with enough cash not to be a burden on the state. Sometimes, I get an unexpected layer of interrogation at the border because I am too tired to perform the gratitude-and-deference dance. In other parts of the world, I am more wary of the chaos. One blink too long and you lose three months of your life as an errant bag skips away into the crowd, or ends up in the wrong country. As I walk through the airport in Port-au-Prince, I am haunted by the memory of the week my luggage and I were separated in Togo: while I disembarked in Lomé, the airline thought my bag needed a quick tour of Benin. Besides, airports generally have too much nervous energy. The last thing I need when arriving in a foreign country I have been warned to be afraid of.

This time, though, my suitcase makes it, and there is no interrogation at the immigration desk. Quite the contrary—the immigration official is pleasantly surprised to see a Kenyan passport. He excitedly tells me that there are quite a few Kenyans in Haiti and I'm surprised but also not surprised: Kenyans tend to travel a lot. There's a restlessness that comes with being Kenyan—a constant centrifugal energy spinning us out into the world at rates that are completely disproportionate to the size of our population. This man is excited that I'm in his country, and that's something—a rare and unexpected reaction from an immigration officer. It does make me breathe a little easier.

My suitcase is heavy and bursting at the seams, yet the smallest one within our group. Porters, most in bright red shirts, bustle around the arrivals hall, looking for *blans*—white people—to help. Of course the "help" is not free, and because I am on a painfully tight budget and still don't know how to negotiate, I am worried about accepting a service that I can't pay for. I worry for a second that someone will grab my bag anyway, but I find I am too dark to pass for anything other than local.

I have been "raced"—my skin colour has created a box, and I am now shoved into it—although for the first time in a while, it actually works in my favour. The porters speak to me in Kreyol, and I have to confess I like it. If I remain silent, I can "pass". There is power in invisibility. I smile dismissively—enough to feign comprehension and communicate that I'm fine. I don't need help carrying my bag—*m'pa blan*. I am not white.

* * *

Edward Said wrote in *After Mahfouz* that "cultures may ... be represented as zones of control or of abandonment, of recollection and of forgetting, of force or of dependence, of exclusiveness or of sharing, all taking place in the global history that is our element. Exile, immigration, and the crossing of boundaries are experiences that can therefore provide us with new narrative forms or, in John Berger's phrase, with *other* ways of telling." Experiences of dislocation and exclusion can give individuals perspective on things that they may take for granted, and a deeper understanding of the fluidity and complexity of culture. Race is one of those elements of culture that travel affects profoundly.

In fact, race is one of the most fascinating constructions of the modern era, and travel has curious ways of throwing up its crude contradictions. We know the science. Biologically, there is little difference between the different human races—slight genotypical and phenotypical differences created due to adaptations for specific climates or environments exist, but we are all fundamentally the same. Yet, because so many cultures are obsessed with categorising both objects and living things, we end up obsessed with real and imagined biological boundaries between various groups. At the extreme, we create academic disciplines that are predicated on hierarchies and exclusion—eugenics, craniometry or anthropology. Groups use their privilege to exact physical and structural violence on others. Less formally, and at the less extreme end, we become determined to prove that our group is different, and the other group less worthy. Human beings seem to default to closed groups, and it takes significant intellect, empathy and intention to open our social and political mindsets and accept others as equal. We make up spurious rules that allow us to conclude that "we" are not like "them".

My summer in Haiti taught me a great deal about the cultural construction of race—perhaps more than I would have learnt just from a classroom. Here I was, black as anyone's business, with curly hair that stood on end to greet the day, but decidedly foreign, in a way that was difficult to contain for people who had learnt everything they knew about Africa from Western media—which was also the source of everything I knew about Haiti. "White" as a short-cut for "privileged" and "other" was repeatedly projected towards me, but it triggered cognitive dissonance in myself and in other people, because it did not correspond at all with my biology. There I was, saddled with inherited fears and misconceptions, while in the circumstances of my visit—an all-expenses-paid trip under the purview of a prestigious American university—my hosts recognised some of the privileges that they associated with whiteness. We each had our unique gazes, but they were both refracted through a lens shaped by Western fears and apprehensions about the black "other".

In recent years, the public has become more aware of something sociologists have articulated for years: that whiteness is a social construction using phenotypical differences to contain privilege. Its logical opposite, blackness, is perhaps better defined as "otherness". On the spectrum of phenotypical differences—skin colour, hair curl, and so on—what is considered "white" in one country might be considered "black" in another. Consider Sudan's "Arab" population. In the political imagination of dictator Omar el-Bashir and his closest advisor Hassan el-Turabi, the basis for Sudan's Arabisation in the early 1990s was a grasp for material and communal support from the alarming wealth the Middle East had accumulated during the 1980s. Sudan's dark-skinned Arabs are, by Western and Middle Eastern measures, black, often on the receiving end of racial slurs when they migrate to the Middle East—*abeed* is a derogatory term that comes from the Arabic word for black. But within Sudan, the "Arab" population distinguishes itself from the country's remaining 150 ethnic groups, often demanding social and political privilege associated with whiteness.

These categories often represent nothing more than a collective desire to create containers for our ideas of privilege and advantage: to give cover to beliefs about worthiness and belonging. Many people have written about this social construction of race, but few as eloquently as Toni Morrison. She said, "The definitions of 'black' and descriptions of what blackness means are so varied and loaded with slippery science and invention that it may be interesting, if not definitively clarifying, to examine the terms' configurations". We often pay so much attention to the categories that power creates that we lose sight of something more interesting: what it says about the people creating the categories. Why, for example, did South Africa's white racist apartheid society need "coloured" people to exist as a distinct social and political category, when similar racist societies in the West simply counted mixed-race people as part of the black population?

Morrison's own expansive views on African and African American literature affirm that she saw something transnational and even transcendental in the way global blackness was created and deployed. But I also love her formulation because it leaves room for specific experiences. She doesn't want to erase the specificity of black experience: to suggest that being black in Brazil is the same as being black in Botswana or being black in Boston. Rather, by starting from the way the concept of black is created—as the logical opposite of the routinely unstated "white"—and then deployed politically, most often to deny people access or privilege, she really shows how groups invented these things for a specific global purpose that moulds itself to local and temporal realities.

Incidentally, I was reading Morrison's *Playing in the Dark* during my time in Haiti. The sum total of my experience there put me directly in contact with the fraying edges of our constructed ideas of race. I am not just black—I am undeniably black, in every society I enter. And African to boot, with a heavy name that twists lazy tongues and announces my African identity to anyone who hears it. But the soft edges of race—where people project privilege based on things that they believe people have, because of their proximity to whiteness—have nothing to do with biology. Standing at the airport, I smiled surreptitiously at the number of people who spoke to me in Kreyol for several heartbeats before taking in the unusual outfit and concluding that there was no way I could be local. A Haitian woman, I was later told, would never be at the airport in loose boyfriend-cut jeans, a faded university tee, dirty black Converse and a hoodie, I was later told. Haitians dress up to go to the airport.

They concluded quickly and correctly that I was "other", but not "other" enough to be white or mixed. Hence the label "*blan*"—literally it means white, but over the next few weeks I would come to realise that it was a figurative descriptor, more of my non-Haitian identity than of the colour of my skin. I would spend a lot of the time in Haiti reaffirming, "*M'pa blan,*" I am not white—because if you're not accustomed to the unearned privilege of racism, it can be a disconcerting experience. "*M'pa blan*" was a declaration of identity that started a process of defining blackness for myself; but one that defined me by what I am not.

We left the airport and headed straight to the mountains for an intensive class in Haitian Creole, or Kreyol. In three days, I hoped to gain enough at least to navigate public transport or taxis on my own. But coming to Haiti had complicated my life—Kreyol was the tenth language I was attempting to squeeze into my brain, and it was getting a little crowded up there—though, thus far, everyone was playing with each other nicely. After the first seven, you begin to notice some patterns. East African languages are all about rhythms—some consonance, others assonance—but, when done right, repetition of syllables or sounds creates a rhythmic lyricism. Latin languages—French, Spanish, Italian—also have a certain lyricism to them, like musical notation hovering over a staff. But their beauty stems in part from their ability to evoke motion or movement by changing intonation, or varying lengths of expression. English, German and other hybrid languages lose a lot of this musicality in favour of a fascinating economy of expression—the form of the word has greater significance, and ever more complex terms become imbued with varying levels of onomatopoeia. What would Kreyol be? What semiotics would this language—a fusion of the Latin lyricism of French, shrunk to the economy of English, and set to the rhythm of long-lost African languages—trigger in my mind?

I experienced a percussive musicality in Kreyol, much as in Kiswahili and my mother-tongue, Banyala; a musical cadence created by the repetition of sounds or variations in intonation. But the instruments that give many East African languages their musicality are not the same instruments. In Swahili there is a reverberating percussion in the repetition of short syllables. (*Hawakukumbukana*—they did not remember each other). In Banyala, the throaty vocals sound like the muffled scratch on a vinyl record. ((*Kh*)*uchakire saa kumi*—we started at ten, where the *kh* sound comes from the back of the throat). In Kreyol there are nasal sounds, borrowed from French and overlaid on an African base. It was familiar, especially because I already understood French by this time, and I had a stronger sense of what each language brings to the mix.

I still get goosebumps when I think about these and other palpable remnants of African identity that remain in Haitian culture. Language is a vector for a shared history, and a vessel for the story of the trans-Atlantic slave trade. The relics are everywhere in the Kreyol language. The use of proverbs to hand down accumulated wisdom. Complex lessons condensed into single phrases that warn of the excesses of greed, ambition or folly. The word *gangan* to mean witchdoctor sounds almost exactly the same as the word *mganga*, which is Swahili for the same. It gave me a sense of being invited in to a secret knowledge that has survived some of the ugliest chapters in human history. Have time, space and place failed to erase the common thread that binds us together? Am I being too essentialist? Probably, but that's the thing with travel and emotions. You can't really predict the direction the emotions will take you or what the experience will bring up in you. In the moment, you let it wash over you, and then later you give yourself time to process it.

I had an interesting Kreyol teacher. He knows more about Haitian history than anyone I've ever met. He is young—maybe the same age as me, maybe a little older. He speaks English, Spanish, Portuguese, Kreyol and French. I mostly feel inadequate when I am in his classroom but I also feel a certain amount of pride. As he stands before our little classroom, passionately unpacking his complex homeland—embracing the flaws and elevating the successes—I feel an inexplicable sense of joy that he's able to command our attention in this way. He believes in Haiti, and his belief and pride in the half-island is contagious: I believe in Haiti too. (I will learn over the next few weeks that this is not a universally held perspective.)

Yet his American boss still speaks to him like a child. I've seen this pattern before. People who claim to be progressive, but still visit poor communities and cannot process equality with the people they find there. It's one thing to preach equality—it's another thing altogether to shun privilege, and the latter takes a tremendous amount of self-awareness and maturity that most people simply don't have. I grow to hate the way she talks to him. It's not out-and-out yelling or abuse. It's just a little micro-aggression here. A snide remark there. A wagged finger in the face. I'm not privy to the complexities of the relationships but I feel ... uneasy. He is one of the best teachers I have ever had—easily. But he is disrespected. Because? He doesn't pay the bills? He doesn't own a car? He works so hard and so well. He deserves more, I think.

I hate it when they roll their eyes behind his back, giggle exasperatedly and say conspiratorially: "That's Haiti." They look at me to participate—I am a foreigner as well. *Me m'pa blan*—but I am not white. "That's Haiti" is truly one of the most offensive things I have ever heard. It is a flag of resignation and despair for people who are trying in the face of unbelievable odds. This is not my conspiracy to participate in. I choose to reject it and therefore I am unfriendly. Cold. Different. Other.

This was to be a recurring theme throughout my time in the country—the energy was different when it was just black people in the room. To be a black man in the world's first black republic to me seems like an exercise in patience and a tutored performance of subservience. To survive in a space like this means constantly bending and adapting to the will of the many NGOs who come to Haiti to "help", because there is just not that much work going outside these organisations. This man who speaks with such certainty and dignity when he is before his class must be coy and uncertain when speaking to the white woman who pays his salary, so as not to appear intimidating or "uppity"—a word with a deep history of racialised violence. He must project a non-threatening demeanour. He can't laugh as robustly as we hear him when he says something that he thinks is hilarious. He can barely sit still. He shuffles around awkwardly, anticipating the next command; forced to look busy even when things are calm. I hate it.

I hate it mostly because I sense that my empowerment as a foreign woman is expected to come at the cost of this man's dignity. He cannot stand at his full metaphorical height: he must slouch a little forward in order to make everyone just a little more comfortable. Privilege like this always comes at someone else's expense.

* * *

I was in Haiti to practise law, itself a frustrating process of learning new languages and forms of expression. Law school was a struggle for me, not because of the content but because of the construct. I had thought I was going to learn how to think about the law and make it work better, but law school was simply training me to be a functionary, a faceless cog in a giant machine that chews up ordinary people to grist its mill. I just wanted to help people, but it felt like most of the time I was being encouraged to help myself. By the time they were my age, I knew, my intellectual heroes had already become firebrand activists: Angela Davis, Steve Biko, Malcolm X, Martin Luther King Jr. I was still a student, buried under deadlines to memorise and regurgitate writing that makes no sense to anyone who hasn't studied the law. Legal writing has no drums or melody. It is dry and caustic. Its only rhythm is the maddening staccato of a frustrated person banging against the sterile, padded white walls in the rooms of an asylum. I still wonder if resistance to the suggestion of madness is what pushed me to Haiti: an attempt to somehow reconnect with the "real world" that law school was encouraging me to leave behind.

Through the project partnering with the local non-profit, I was to work with juvenile victims of rape. This involved supporting a network of victims in Port-au-Prince, Haiti as well as the groups that represent them. After the 2010 earthquake that destroyed much of Port-au-Prince, many Haitian families and individuals had moved to temporary tent cities, living in tight closed quarters with insufficient humanitarian support. For young girls and women, the vulnerability to sexual assault multiplied. The predators came in many forms—strangers, family members, religious leaders, aid workers and peacekeepers. Thin walls hold few secrets, and because many of the perpetrators were known to the victims and their families, the victims then had to live with or near their abusers. Many were dealing with a great deal of shame. This shame in part explained their unwillingness to seek help from formal legal and judicial mechanisms, which were already lax in applying the laws prohibiting rape but now, overwhelmed by the scale of the tragedy, simply did not have the capacity to do the work. This little project was trying to change that by providing a safe space where the victims could speak openly about their lives—not just their assaults; where family members could receive group counselling; and where some of the country's bright young lawyers could help prosecute cases.

The thing about change in life is that it often comes when you least expect it. I am ashamed to admit that I didn't go into this work expecting the profound transformation that I experienced. Ninety-five per cent of the women that we worked with were actually girls—they were all minors when they were raped. The youngest were 3 years old when the attack happened, and all their rapists were over the age of 50. As I read the case files, trying to put together aggregate statistics, I felt like I was being repeatedly punched in the stomach or being shaken, emotionally weighed down. Violence has a very powerful toxicity—it contaminates anything that comes into contact with it. So much so that even reading about the violence done to these young girls poisoned my spirit, and it made me violently ill.

They're just babies.

At one point, I thought I had malaria—I didn't. My spirit was just beaten down. I needed to do something differently. I needed to find a new way of dealing with the violence that was contained in those case files. For me the solution turned out to be quite simple. Contrary to what they teach you as the fundamentals of lawyering, I decided to get to know as many of my clients as possible. To become invested in them as human beings, and as more than the total of the violence they had experienced. It turned out to be the right call.

Once a week, the practice would gather all our victims at our office for a support session. Generally, this was an incredibly positive space—the girls learnt new skills. They talked to each other, not as victims, but as survivors. They were warm, kind, funny and incredibly generous to a clumsy foreigner for whom Home Economics was kryptonite. They were helping me with my Kreyol and teaching me how to crochet. I was teaching them to laugh at and with foreigners without feeling a need to be overly deferential. I was learning to make myself small enough to claim whatever little room I could find in their imagination for a connection with a person from a faraway place.

I met an amazing girl who was 9 when she was raped and impregnated by her brother. Her name means Beauty. Appropriate, because she has an inner beauty that scorches any shyness or insecurity on my part. She throws herself into everything with the force of a tropical storm. She giggled and talked to her best friend while the sessions were in progress, charming me with a beautiful smile when I asked her to stop. She loved to stand next to me after the sessions and I think it's because there I was, a foreigner but not quite: in a place of relative authority, but with the same deeply dark skin as hers.

One Saturday, she brought her baby with her to the session. Have you ever held a baby in your hands and just sensed that something was wrong? When I looked into her eyes, I saw a vast desert that I was not certain I could cross. The baby's reactions were slow and her face was neither hard nor soft: it just had this vacancy that most people only develop after years of disappointment. She didn't laugh, smile or cry. She lived in a world that comes close to but doesn't quite overlap with ours. I have no doubt that her mother and grandmother love this beautiful, different baby. Because she was not unique in this space, the Saturday group gave Beauty a chance to be a teenager without shaming her into hiding her baby. In fact, everyone wanted to hold her. Beauty could still laugh and get excited about the summer camp we were organising, even if she had to walk away for a bit to feed the baby that her body had probably been too young to carry.

This is maybe the part where I should share some profound lessons about gratitude that I got from this experience. I did learn, but not in the linear "Thank God I don't have those problems" straw through which we are often expected to imbibe other people's experiences or struggle. People don't suffer so that we, the relatively privileged, can grow, as spectators to other people's pain. More than anything, in Haiti I learnt about resilience and empathy, and how to turn that into a political practice. bell hooks writes beautifully about love as political practice in her book *All About Love: New Visions*. She articulates love for all people regardless of their proximity to you. Embedded in this practice of love is a desire for justice, truth-telling, respect, commitment, spirituality—or a desire to connect with the spiritual in the other person—and other values that move our political behaviour as humanitarians away from pity and condescension, towards a desire for a just and equitable world. It's not about helping people because we feel bad for them, but helping people because we want them to experience the same fullness of life that we ourselves aspire to.

Those Saturday meetings forced me to think about the place of love, and its product, empathy, in what I wanted my professional life to look like. I had always been uncomfortable with the depersonalisation that legal practice was encouraging me to embrace, and over the weeks I was in Haiti I finally saw that there could be a different way. Those girls taught me that I didn't need to put myself on a pedestal to be able to earn their attention and respect. I just had to be honest, just and committed. The connections that I had been grasping at throughout my stay gave me a crutch to start reframing my own ethics of practice.

I think what helped the most was something that I initially did out of necessity. One thing they never warn you about when you go to work overseas from a place of relative privilege is the gilded cage you will live in: holed up in the leafy suburbs, forbidden from using public transport, unable to access local life, confined to the gated communities and their never-ending cycles of dinner parties. With the victims' network, meetings were held on Saturdays, but we foreign volunteers did not have access to a driver on weekends. So I walked to the meetings every Saturday—3 kilometres downhill, 3 kilometres uphill—in Port-au-Prince's stifling humidity. Honestly, it wasn't a profound decision on my part. I needed to get there, and I didn't have access to a car. And at this point, I needed to be with the group probably more than they needed me. I was getting cabin fever, but I also needed to experience the human experiences behind the case files—to give the secondary trauma purpose—perhaps more than they needed me and my faltering Kreyol.

Showing up matters. I think showing up sweaty and a little dusty every Saturday signalled a sense of commitment that I was willing to do this every week just to be with them. An Indigenous women's rights activist once said, "If you have come to save me, you are wasting your time. But if you have come because your liberation is bound up with mine, then let us struggle together." I have this phrase seared into my conscious and subconscious because of Haiti. Haiti taught me to walk with the people that I was claiming to help, rather than observe them from an abstract and removed distance. I still had to learn boundaries. I still needed to set aside space for my own sanity, through travel to other parts of the island or long walks to other parts of Port-au-Prince, just to clear my head. But the small difference that it made to be with the group on those Saturday mornings has left an indelible mark on my political practice. I can't claim to always get it right, but I try to keep it embedded in the work that I do—let us struggle together. Let us build together, because we all need each other so we can be okay.

* * *

One week, the group asks me to speak—with the help of a translator—about the state of women's rights in Kenya. At first, I am not keen, because my Kreyol is still pretty terrible, especially for such a big topic, and my French is still not perfect. I am equally concerned about the age range: teenagers get bored and can make you feel like you're the worst thing in the world. Then I remembered reading about "theatre of the oppressed" as an advocacy tool from a friend working with Dalit women in India. I decide to try it.

The premise of theatre of the oppressed is simple—using theatre to flip the script on power dynamics that lead to oppression by giving the power to the oppressed. First, we learnt a simple Swahili song, to place Kenya in a broader global context. The delight with which the girls worked at learning the song made me wonder if they sensed the familiarity of the language, the same way I had in my Kreyol class. We then did some theatre exercises to loosen up and get into a more open headspace. My goal was to build trust with the girls, and create whatever rudimentary form of rapport we could in the gulf of language and culture between us. My blackness was an asset in this context. Although my unfamiliarity with the language clearly alienated me, the girls were more forgiving with my lapses and less guarded than they had been. In the following stage, the group that you are advocating for gets to put together a scenario in which they feel that their power is undermined or taken away from them. I asked the girls to show me, through theatre, what it felt like to be walking through their neighbourhoods and their schools: how did the boys and men react to them? What did they say?

If the familiar rhythms of Kreyol make me happy, the familiar rhythms of harassment and violence endured by the girls of Port-au-Prince break my heart. Their dramatic sketches matched, beat for beat, my own and other women's experiences of navigating public space in Nairobi. The men and boys in their homes approach their femininity with the same violence and aggression

I see in New York, in London, in Nairobi, in Kinshasa. Even without fully understanding the language, I could detect the forcefulness with which males demand their attention. I almost forgot they were children when I saw the subtlety with which they captured these power dynamics. One of the girls, who I normally viewed as sweet and shy, was unrestrained when embodying a young man unhappy with her rejection of his advances. These girls were tired of being afraid. They were ready to be seen as people.

I think about this global tapestry of oppression that women live under: when we are still far too young, we have to learn how to navigate the violence and excesses of men. These little girls have to learn, even while their ages are still in single digits, how to make themselves almost invisible, just to walk safely through their own neighbourhoods. Women, even before they stop being girls, must develop an entire extra set of skills that have no function other than protecting themselves from men. I think of all the hours we spend subconsciously learning all these strategies and then applying them: what would women accomplish if they didn't have to spend so much energy learning how to survive men? How far would we get if we didn't have to carry this extra burden? There are very few women in the world who don't grow up with this pressure.

In the next stage, the performers repeat the scene, but this time the non-performing audience has to interact. Basically, whenever the rest of the group sees something that makes them unhappy, they have to stop the action by yelling: "Stop!" At that point, I, as the "Joker", ask them to explain what it is they didn't like, and why. Then I ask them to change the scene to how they would want it to be. Finally, we replay the whole thing, with the adaptations they have introduced. To run the session I only had to memorise a handful of Kreyol lines—"Stop! What didn't you like? What would you change? Okay, now repeat it." I drew upon my experience as a teacher and teaching assistant to instruct without intimidating.

I sensed that the girls really appreciated the chance to speak. Lawyers, more so than any other professionals, rely on their ability to dominate conversations in order to assert their intellectual or moral superiority. We are taught to command dialogue in courtrooms and to guide conversations to where we want them. Add racial, age and gender hierarchies to the mix and, in a society like the one I found in Haiti, these young girls are practically at the bottom of the food chain. I can only imagine how their regular interactions with lawyers have coloured their experiences of the profession.

In my pre-law work, I found that the most powerful thing you can do is to cede space, and give people who are vulnerable room to vent what's on their mind. Your job is just to listen. Theatre of the oppressed made it easier for me to listen, despite the language barriers. In listening, I saw many of the girls in a new light, one I suspect few of their lawyers had seen before. They threw themselves into the performance, and I learnt a great deal about what their lives are like.

At the end of an exhilarating session, I found myself wondering about privilege and the nature of advocacy, and especially how far current models of international advocacy are premised on leveraging the privilege of those who claim to be advocates, rather than on giving people the tools they need to advocate for themselves. I have never used the noun "advocate" to just mean "lawyer". I think a lawyer is someone who has the technical skills to represent someone in a courtroom or in a legal matter. But an advocate is someone who speaks up for and with other people in the face of power. That was the traditional meaning of the word before the legal profession co-opted it. And because advocacy is necessarily about confronting power, the identity of the advocate can be important—and harmful if we don't pay it enough attention.

Consider the idea of goodwill ambassadors or co-opting celebrity culture into campaigns. Using a famous person to bring attention to lesser-known causes is supposed to be helpful, but sometimes it does more harm than good. When we use people's lives and stories merely to invoke pity, we dehumanise them. We flatten them. We define the sum total of their experiences as the suffering they have endured. "There's really no such thing as the 'voiceless'. There are only the deliberately silenced, or the preferably unheard", says Arundhati Roy. I thought about this statement a lot while I was in Haiti. What was my place, in claiming to be an advocate, in deliberately un-hearing individuals, communities and societies? And how could I do things differently?

The legal advocacy to which I had been exposed by this time focuses so much on developing the rhetorical or legal skills of the advocate, and so little on teaching the advocate to listen and create space for the advocated-for. As a law student—particularly as a black, female law student in one of the most prestigious law schools in the world—I was taught that I have power and that I must assert it. I have to take up as much room as I possibly can. Yet as an advocate, I sensed that I am much more useful and effective in my silence than in my speech; that the real power in building strong communities is in giving others the power to build them. I was empowered, but conflicted. Is there room for this kind of advocacy in the law?

* * *

As Edward Said put it in his essay *Identity, Authority and Freedom*, "The world we live in is made up of numerous identities interacting, sometimes harmoniously, sometimes antithetically. Not to deal with that whole ... is not to have academic freedom. We cannot make our claim as seekers after justice that we advocate knowledge only of and about ourselves. Our model for academic freedom should therefore be the migrant or traveler..." The traveller, in other words, can be a template for untethered intellectual curiosity, and an example of what freedom is created by certain forms of mobility.

As time passed, the caricatured image that I had of Haiti fell away; something closer to intellectual freedom—the freedom to redefine myself—was taking shape. Everything that I learnt about Haiti before I arrived had been filtered through the US mindset. By the end, I was learning more and more every day that I knew nothing. This peace in unknowing was the profound shift that I hadn't known I was looking for. After close to a decade in higher education at some of the best universities in the world, I had come to Haiti and learnt something interesting at the intersection of power and knowledge.

There are things that we know with our minds, and things we know with our spirits. There are things that we hear in the grammar of language and histories that are buried in its morphology and sentences. My unknowing had opened up a new way of thinking and being: after so many years of leading with my mind, I felt like I was finally reaching towards a balance of some kind—letting this other part of my self reach into the world.

In place of the intellectual certainty that had brought me to Haiti came an increasing understanding of the challenges of identity. Haitians are constructing a post-colonial identity in a space where the originally colonised inhabitants of Hispaniola— the Taino—have long since been destroyed, and where all that is left is a legacy of revolution and counter-revolution. In Kenya, we know that if we strip away the British Puritanism or the Islamic winds from the coast, there is a myriad of African identities jostling for dominance and survival. What about Haiti? Who are the Haitians underneath French colonisation, US invasion, Dominican racism and African counter-revolution, now that the Taino are gone?

I latched onto one of the new ways of understanding that travel has opened to me. Before leaving for Port-au-Prince, I had bought a DSLR camera, hoping not so much for a latent artistry, but to document whatever strange mysteries the country held in store. Now, a mission formed. I decided to tell a new story of contemporary Haiti through my photography, going out of my way to seek out the most unusual or unreported elements of the island nation's identity. I was not trying to be good; I was trying to be present, and photography helps me do that by forcing me to stop and think about what I am seeing and not seeing. I was determined not to be afraid of Haiti, so I spent many weekends walking through the streets of my neighbourhood in Pacot, in other parts of Port-au-Prince, or even in Cap-Haïtien, capturing as much of the country as I could with my new tool. These pictures tell a more powerful story than any words I could have strung together in the heat of the summer. My writing mind was content to relax while my seeing mind experimented with this new way of experiencing the world.

My first photoset explores the abandoned houses and swimming pools of Pacot, a neighbourhood formerly home to Baby Doc Duvalier and now dotted with abandoned mansions, as many of the elite opted not to reconstruct after the 2010 earthquake. We lived in Pacot because we were told that it was safe, but the juxtaposition of our little yellow apartment complex with the mosquito-infested waters of the cracked swimming pool next door is a reminder of the futility of materiality. There are some things against which even the highest walls cannot protect. A little down the road, the walls of Baby Doc's mansion were still cracked and collapsed, and a uniformed guard chewing on a single blade of grass barely looked at me as I stopped and stared at the walls on my walk past.

I catalogued Haiti's glorious gingerbread houses voraciously. Indeed, over the summer, these architectural curiosities became a mild obsession for me. Built in the early twentieth century, they are, in my imagination, a testament to Haitian ingenuity and resilience. They are one of the things that too many people un-see about this fascinating country. Perfectly attuned to the vagaries of the weather, they seem to mock the concrete rubble that still dots parts of Port-au-Prince; imposing wooden structures rising above the rock. In the 1800s, houses in Port-au-Prince were mostly made of wood, because the inhabitants knew that the island was susceptible to earthquakes. These beautiful, grand homes are built for Port-au-Prince, with large shuttered windows that allow whatever cooling breeze caresses the island to move effortlessly through, without retaining any of the oppressive heat. Two powerful earthquakes have come and gone, but the gingerbread houses remain standing, magnificent and imposing in a city that has been ridiculed in travel guides for being chaotic and boring. The only parts that succumbed to the force of the earthquake were those that ignored the historic specifications during renovations, and replaced the gingerbread with inflexible concrete.

The symbolism haunted my stay in Haiti. Every time I saw one of these houses, I thought: what if Haiti were allowed to exist on its own terms? Would it be more resilient if it were allowed to build itself with materials that made sense for it, rather than for US whims? What if, when we rebuilt Haiti, instead of forcing our vision or view of the world on the island nation, we rebuilt in a way that was sensitive to the local conditions? What if, instead of bringing in our political ideas crafted in think-pieces and classrooms, we listened for ideas that are vulnerable to the unusual challenges of culture, history or community in the country? What if we listened to the Haitian people, and tried to do things their way first? What would that listening look like? How could we guarantee that we were hearing the right voices and not just the loudest ones? This haunting changed the way I worked—I became consumed with listening to our victims' network, and fell behind on implementing the many plans that I received from head office. I became impatient with myself and other people—could they not see that I was a work in progress? Growth, I found, is an awkward, painful and uncomfortable process.

As the weeks went by, the narrative of despair that I've heard from others who have been in Haiti no longer jived with the exciting, but admittedly complicated, story that was unfolding in my photography. Could a "backwards" nation produce some of the most compelling street art that I have seen in decades? How could I reconcile the story of the failing state with the majesty of the Citadel in Cap-Haïtien? How do we acknowledge the very real struggles that Haitians face every day because of the structures of oppression and poverty, without dismissing the brilliance, creativity and genius of what is and what went before? And, personally, how could I legitimise my role as an aid worker when I no longer believed that the country needed the help I came to offer? I set out to find a Haitian identity through my photography, and what I found was a place defined and redefined by others for many long years; a country where "development" practice was simply another ill-informed and inadequate way of making sense of the complex national identity.

I shared my photographs with my friends on Facebook and on my blog, and my albums were perpetually met with surprise: "That's Haiti" became "This is Haiti?" The Otherness that led to racial abuse on the subway in New York and in the side streets of Boston had given me an inroad that seemed inaccessible to my *blan* colleagues. I was able to walk through the streets and take photographs in relative security; I was much more quickly able to access a Haiti that is warm and welcoming, rather than strange and fearful. Even when I spoke, my Africanness put people at ease. Privilege is funny that way. People, when they learn that I am African, almost always assume that they have had a better life than I have. A black, African woman is almost always at the bottom of whatever constructed hierarchy of value a society has in place, and so I am more likely to be viewed as an object of pity than as a target for theft or bribery.

It is of course complicated. Black people rarely control the images they receive about other black communities around the world, or that are projected about them. The Haitian view of Africa is no exception. The "poor Africa" narrative pervaded most of my in-depth interactions there. My identity—educated, African, well-travelled, single—made no sense in this framework, and I could sense that many of the Haitian people I met were struggling to find a box for me. I encountered some troubling self-loathing—"That's Haiti" is a thing that some Haitians believe about themselves. One colleague, linking the abject poverty he imagines in Africa with the struggles of Haiti, asked me if struggle is predicated by the colour of our skin. "Are black people just bad at things?" he suggested, and I snapped. I argued passionately, in halting Kreyol, that there is more to Africa, and indeed to Haiti, than poverty and struggle. We are bigger than what we hear about each other. He left the room, clearly unconvinced, and I remained, thinking about the power of the stories we believe about ourselves.

By the end of my stay in Haiti, the path to professional satisfaction had grown blurry. I wanted to help, but I was no longer clear on what that help would look like. For one, I was convinced that the biggest problem facing contemporary Haiti was its proximity to the US. Fanon made his anti-imperialist case in part by urging a national consciousness, which subsequently transforms into a social consciousness "as soon as the withdrawal of the coloniser has been accomplished". But Haiti's contemporary coloniser doesn't seem willing to withdraw, and the connections are only getting more pervasive and complicated. How can decolonisation begin when you have a neighbour with an unapologetic imperialist streak? How can Haitians build a social consciousness when every story they hear about themselves is told with the intention of keeping them down?

In such situations, growth of a national identity infused with pride and dignity is suffocated and stunted by the imposition of outmoded or ill-suited methods of thinking about progress and development. Then there is the harm we do to ourselves, through corruption and inefficiencies that come from generations of proxy governments. And aid workers are part of the problem. Organisations that encourage creativity and ingenuity are starved for funds and attention; institutions that are bogged down by bureaucracy and short-sightedness are rolling in cash, but unable to deploy it where it is needed the most. And the people get stuck in the middle. We the "beneficiaries"—the aid recipients, the Others—find that every aspect of our existence has always to be geared towards "development", and anything that gives us joy in its purest forms—music, dance, art, food— becomes a luxury.

In Haiti, I was unlearning so many things that were core to my professional aspirations and identity. But I still didn't know what I would do next.

* * *

"Being black is not a matter of pigmentation—being black is a reflection of a mental attitude ... Merely by describing yourself as black you have started on a road towards emancipation, you have committed yourself to fight against all forces that seek to use your blackness as a stamp that marks you out as a subservient being." Steve Biko's words are fresh in my mind as I start to process my departure from Haiti.

One of my last tasks is to organise a needs assessment with all the representatives from our victims' rights network. Instead of a long, detailed questionnaire, I decide to convene a roundtable with women's rights leaders and ask three simple questions: what problems do you face as women in Haiti? What problems do you face as group leaders in Haiti? What solutions do you see to these problems? I am careful not to ask, "How can I help?", because I don't want my own presence to cloud the conversation, or to dangle an illusion of power that I don't have. Once again, I am blown away by the ability of the women to articulate a struggle that translates across the language limitations. These things are so painfully familiar to any woman. There are tears, sighs of frustration, and that universal handclap that black women often use to express exasperation.

I am unsure what I can do to help these organisations beyond bringing them to the attention of my superiors, of outsiders and of anyone who will listen. Haitians, I have learnt, are itching to be given the reins in their own country. It seems that there really are some problems you can fix simply by throwing more money at them. Haitians need more funds—not strings-attached charity, or microcredit-style money that turns them into indentured labourers. Just money that goes directly to the people who need it the most. Call it reparations; call it compensation for decades of interference.

As for me, I leave with more questions than answers on what it means to be an advocate. We come to help, but as soon as we turn up, we do something to the water. And I don't just mean the cholera that the UN introduced to Haiti in the wake of the earthquake. We say, "I am an advocate," and thus claim power. We change the way people relate to each other. We build our gated communities on sacred hills and in protected forests to guard against the danger that apparently accompanies whiteness in poor black or brown places. We foreigners come to "help" but then hide behind our fear in earmarked neighbourhoods, zipping around in four-wheel drives with tinted windows, sighing our pity at the huddled masses and pausing every few days to remember to be grateful that "at least it's not us". We remain high on the hills where the air is fresh and clear, and where we can safely sneer at the people below.

"That's Haiti," we mumble as we order that second glass of imported whiskey with ice made from mineral water.

None of this is a judgement on people who make the decision to go. It is more a reflection that choices do indeed have consequences, and the entire international advocacy paradigm requires some critical reflection. Advocacy as practised in much of the world today is loaded with Biko's concept of "whiteness" as the antithesis of "blackness". It is a world of power, privilege and decadence. To be *blan* in Haiti is to drink, dance and holiday in places where the ordinary Haitians cannot reach you. It makes it "impossible to get around", even though the roads are congested with *blokis*—traffic jams—from the too-many cars and motorcycles, squeezed on roads too narrow for the amount of traffic they see. "Too dangerous," I am cautioned, and I agree. Except, Haitians have to use them; they have to get places too. How can we conceivably help if we are too good for the lives of the people we came to help?

Blan money brings in imports that the locals can't afford to eat and cars we won't let them drive. I understand fear. I cultivate a healthy respect for it and modify my behaviour accordingly. Should I feel guiltier about my large box of American cookies? What about the box of herbal tea? Am I any better because I choose to walk, a compromise between the zipping around on a moto and never leaving home? Is this all okay because I came to help? I see so much to criticise but feel less prone to criticising: I am no better than those I would challenge. I take pictures that I probably shouldn't take. I am afraid of the water coming from my tap. I surreptitiously glance over my shoulder when I am on my long, lonely walks.

I want to be different, but I don't know how. Travel has a way of throwing everything into relief, contrasted, saturated and searing in its starkness—including Biko's blackness, always ascribed to me, with or without my acceptance. When I travel, I am more aware of my blackness; my womanhood; my age; my Africanness; the dense, impenetrable curl of my hair. *Blans* do not see me. Haitians do not see me. I am background, regardless of who is looking. Yet, an advocate should never be invisible. There can be a certain kind of power in invisibility, yes, but there is disempowerment in it too. There is risk in not being able to use your privilege to get succour on demand.

Still, the food tastes familiar. I hear the African rhythm underneath the French lyricism in Kreyol as it rolls across Haitian tongues. No one in Haiti asks if they can touch my hair—it is not a mystical thing that requires further investigation. I can buy shampoo at a regular supermarket. I can sit at a bus stop and wait for a taxi without drawing unnecessary attention. I belong more here than I ever have on the streets of Cambridge, Massachusetts. I take inexplicable offence for Haiti when people call her "backward", "difficult", "incomprehensible"—I adapt. My blackness—visible, indelible, undeniable, constructed and laced with imputed meaning—is somehow staking a claim for me in Haiti, with or without my help. I become.

Several weeks later, I leave. I walk through the airport with more confidence, because I have learnt enough Kreyol to navigate the space and politely decline the porter's help. I can laugh over simple things with the people I meet at the airport. I feel bigger in unprecedented ways, even though I am deeper in unknowing this day than the day I arrived. For one, I have no idea what the next phase of my professional life will look like—I am going back to law school without a plan. I leave with no answers; just many questions, and an odd sense of kinship and relief. Haiti isn't the awful scary place that some of the preparatory material wanted me to believe. It's just a place, like any other place, full of people trying to make a way in the face of complicated odds. And I am living a cliché—I came to help change Haiti, but I am the one who ends up transformed.

2

TRAVELLING WHILE BLACK

The pitch black night of the Sahara does not yield to the sunlight until it is good and ready, and when it does, it flees so fast
that you would think the place is constantly bathed in blinding
light. Stark sunrises turn the giant dunes dull brown for a scant
few seconds; for a handful of minutes, as the sun is creeping up
the sky, the sand glows. Then the sky cracks fully open and
turns brilliant blue, and everything around you will shimmer in
response. Until that moment when the blue scares off the dark,
the dusty roads leading from Gorom-Gorom to Oursi, a small
town outside a small town in northern Burkina Faso, are
shrouded in the desert's secrecy, blanketed by inscrutable darkness and breathtaking silence. Six nights a week, that is.

From the small hours of the seventh night, on Thursday
mornings, the twilight is split open by a convoy of traders from
across the Sahara—on foot, horses, camels or caravans—quietly
inching towards the small desert town. These are people heading
silently to the weekly market: women with baskets and buckets
balanced on their heads out front, and in the rear the regal families undulating on their camels, the women dressed to the nines

in brilliant white, with all their glittering silver and gold bridal wealth, and the men draped in indigo-dyed tunics. Later, I would watch residents of the town providing water for the animals with no payment expected, and travellers setting up mats and blankets under the awnings of the homes and shops lining the main street, to shelter from the blistering afternoon sun. This spectacle alone was worth every single dollar that I had spent crossing Togo, then Ghana and finally Burkina Faso. And to think that I nearly missed it because I was afraid.

Fear is a powerful and paralysing impulse. In healthy doses, it can protect us from being a danger to ourselves and to others. In unhealthy doses, it can be the difference between living a rich, fulfilling life or ending your life as an anecdote in one of those "regrets of the dying" articles. And whatever fears you have in your normal life—spiders, snakes, regret, heartbreak—are only intensified by travel, giving even the simplest choices a heavy patina of urgency.

I like to think of my trip to Gorom-Gorom and other parts of Burkina Faso as the first in a series of lessons on the nature of fear and the rewards of confronting it. It was my first truly solo and completely spontaneous trip. After a disappointing six weeks in Togo and a fulfilling six in Ghana, I had found myself with ten days to spend on anything I wanted to do. I needed a plan. I could have stayed in Ghana and hung out while my friends worked, but I was itching for a challenge, and I wasn't sure at that time if I would ever go back to West Africa again. So I did something I had never done before, but now do regularly: I pulled out a map, looked at the countries surrounding Ghana and almost randomly picked a place to go.

And went.

I was terrified at every step of my trip to Burkina Faso. When I was buying my bus ticket I wondered if they were cheating me. When I had to get on the bus I was afraid that it would crash.

When I was on the bus I was scared that the people sitting next to me would try and steal from me. When we crossed the border and encountered a platoon of soldiers training, I thought there had been a coup. When I got into Ouagadougou I was afraid of getting lost or mugged. When I bought my ticket to Gorom-Gorom, near the border with Mali, I was petrified of getting kidnapped. The list of things that could have made me turn around and go back at any point was so unbearably long, and I was just constantly afraid for things that I had never even seen. I had this cloud of trepidation weighing on every step I tried to take, and every breath felt like a battle against my own mind.

These are the things that the guidebooks tell you to be afraid of, and I had read all the guidebooks religiously, not realising that I wasn't the target market for those particular guidebooks, and that those fears were being refracted through a very specific life experience. It wasn't until I went to Burkina Faso that I fully appreciated how important our identities are to the ways we experience the world and, more importantly, to the way our conversations about fear and travel are framed. We consume information about each other surreptitiously and passively, and form stereotypes and judgements around other people, not realising that they are doing the same to us. Until I went to Burkina Faso I didn't fully appreciate that, as a black African woman with a smattering of French, I could have an experience that the guidebooks couldn't really see.

Every time I pushed through another mental barrier, I grew more certain of a philosophy that was slowly taking shape in my mind. Fear is never a good reason not to do something. Up to this point, I think I'd believed that if you were afraid of something, it meant it wasn't good for you to do that something, and you were better off staying close to the shore. But as each challenge was overcome and a new beautiful mystery of Burkina Faso revealed itself, I started to experience the immense rewards of using fear as a catalyst for action, rather than a deterrent. Fear can give us rational boundaries that protect us from excess. But it can also be crippling. The trick is figuring out which fears are worth keeping and which fears are worth pushing past.

There was no plan when I arrived in Ouagadougou. That was the first major difference between this trip and all the other trips I had taken to that point. "You're supposed to have a plan!" is what the books say—make a plan, work the plan. But a plan can quickly become a crutch that makes it impossible for you to discover what weight you can carry on your own. A plan can be a misguided effort at absolute control, in a world where absolute control is never really guaranteed. A plan can shield you from the wonderful joys of discovery.

Initially, I was only supposed to spend ten days experiencing Ouagadougou, but as I grew more comfortable strolling through the broad boulevards and listening to the harmattan sand blasting the roof of the convent where I was staying, the urge to see more of the country grew. The guidebook said Gorom-Gorom was once in a lifetime, and I was desperate for once in a lifetime; so I bought the bus ticket and went, hoping that I would figure out the accommodation situation once I got there. And this was my second lesson: once you taste the rewards of pushing against the boundaries of your own fears, you want that feeling again and again.

That doesn't mean that the fears went away. The morning of the drive to Gorom-Gorom, I woke up at 6 a.m. and walked through the city towards the bus station, with my giant backpack and sleeping bag on my back. In my head, I might as well have been carrying a flag saying, "Hello, I'm a tourist—please rob me?" Recall that everything I knew about West Africa up to this point had surreptitiously agreed that it was mysterious, scary and teeming with bodies lurking in the shadows, waiting to rob you. Remember Robert Kaplan's much-touted essay "The Coming

Anarchy" (1994)? Guidebooks are written with such sweeping certainty that it never occurred to me that I might find something different from what their authors had documented.

Yet as I walked through the streets of the city that morning, I noticed that no one was noticing me. Traders sweeping the sidewalk before their days began and office workers shuffling towards their desk jobs milled past me, so focused on their own journeys that I was merely another obstacle in their path. I was someone they had to walk around or dodge but not really acknowledge. No one was even looking at me. I was just another person on the street with something to do and somewhere to go.

How glorious! The discovery that I could be invisible made it possible for me to relax fully into the role of observer. I realised that, if I said nothing, everyone would presume that I was local and let me get on with my business, much as they went on with theirs. That uncomfortable feeling you get when you go to a new place—that everyone is watching you—I didn't have that. And I could breathe.

This was how I started to appreciate that, because I had been uncritically consuming other people's versions of Africa—shaped by particulars of those people's existence—I had learnt to be afraid of it. This was reflected quietly in the way that I thought about the horizons of possibility, of what I thought was wrong or troubling about the continent, and what needed to be changed. Later, I would go back to my travel guides and realise something that today seems so painfully obvious: the vast majority of guidebooks, especially those written about Africa, are written by white men for white men. Does this matter? It shouldn't, but of course it does. It is an unfortunate consequence of the world that we have built, and until we all develop the moral clarity to move away from it, it matters.

Race (like gender, sexuality and other markers of identity) shapes travel—and backpacking especially—in such palpable ways. As a black woman, there are spaces where my race and gender make me invisible, which means that I can immerse myself more fully into the lives of those around me. And there are spaces where it makes me hyper-visible, like taking the train from Vienna to Bern and being the only people in our full carriage who get their identity documents checked.

My guidebooks, with all their warnings of violent thugs and itchy fingers, need their presumed readers to be afraid of Africa. They are written for people who have a significant amount of privilege and power, more than most of the people in the communities they plan to enter. This presumption of wealth and power—that privilege will precede these white men travelling outside Europe—also makes them a target for the kind of crimes that the guidebooks warn about. Privilege can insulate the traveller from consequences, but it can also make someone a lightning rod for unwanted attention. It's the difference between Europeans who get to beg and panhandle their way through South-East Asia visa-free, and Nigerians who have to provide a laundry list of requirements including a letter from their father just to apply for a visa to Thailand or Indonesia.

Burkina Faso reminded me that I had no reason to borrow the fears of others wholesale. It was a little crazy for me to be just as—if not more—afraid of the people of Burkina Faso than any of the French tourists I encountered on the trip. Fear is subjective, and each subject must order their fears based on their own reality. This doesn't mean that I always feel safe when backpacking—invisibility cuts both ways. I still carry a fear that if something bad should happen to me, there would be no hue and cry, because the world doesn't stop turning for missing or dead black women in the way it does for white men and women. Being black in Africa is not an invitation to take stupid risks. But it does mean that people's assumptions cut in your favour in a way that they just don't elsewhere.

Backpacking in Burkina Faso taught me to stop being afraid of this invisibility and chase after the opportunities it offers. The same energy that confounds and terrifies visitors to Africa, keeping them away from the pulsing, chaotic heart of many of its towns and cities, has given me some of the most memorable experiences of my life. Embracing fear, listening to it but refusing to cow to it, has nurtured my love for backpacking; and backpacking has given me the world.

3

A THOUSAND WORDS

In a stirring dirge for victims of a lynching, Billie Holiday mourns the strange fruit borne by Southern trees. She laments the blood pooling on the leaves and at the roots, with the haunting image of black bodies swinging in the breeze. Centuries of desperation, frustration, and anger over racial crimes and injustices are distilled into the song, in which a raw vocal pours over the simple strains of three chords: a hollowed-out musical structure that echoes the moral vacuum in which lynching became common in America's South. "Strange Fruit" reveals perfectly the true power of art. By stripping superfluity and presenting the ugly, it cuts through your heart; what remains is devastating to the core and impossible to deny.

I thought about this song when I saw the jarring pictures of the bodies of 3-year-old Alan Kurdi and his 5-year-old brother Galip, who washed up dead near a tourist resort on the Turkish coast. In a series of disturbing pictures, photographer Nilüfer Demir captured the moment the bodies of the two boys and their mother, Rehan—all Syrian refugees fleeing the devastation in Kobani by crossing the Mediterranean Sea on a flimsy boat—

washed onto shore. The image of Alan's lifeless form in particular sparked public conversations about whether photos of a child
should be taken and shared without the consent of their guard-
ians; whether sharing these photographs is cruel voyeurism; and
what it says about the state of humanity that a genuine conversation on intervening in Syria can only be had once the public is
confronted by a waterlogged and lifeless infant body.

Images are powerful precisely because they distil so much
social complexity and upheaval into a single moment, and their
impact can outlast both the person who makes the image, and
the society they have made it for. A single photograph contains
multiple stories—about the image, the image-maker, and the
people who consume the image. It can condense chaos, but it
can also create chaos. A photograph can develop a life outside the
moment of its creation when it intersects with power and politics, and when the intent of the artist is scrutinised. The final
analysis is about not just what is contained in a photograph, but
also what is missing—who gets photographed, how are they
staged, whose photographs survive in the archive. What makes a
natural subject for a photographic series and what context must
be contained—all of this is a contentious discourse of power that
has haunted photography ever since the first daguerreotypes were
taken in the 1840s.

Photographs are powerful tools for people working in advocacy around migration justice because the more debates have
become loaded with the vulgar demands of competitive politics,
the more the simple premises have been lost. The more individuals in parliaments and state houses make abstract claims about
immigrants stealing jobs and bringing diseases, the more
removed the conversation becomes from its context, particularly
when the advocates take on the language of power to try and
defend those people on the move. Power sets the tone for the
debate, and the advocates go along with it, and photographs like

Alan Kurdi's then become important moments for resetting the debate and remembering that we are talking about people who need help urgently.

But the use of photographs in this way also forces an audit on the values of the image-maker and image-consumer alike. Photographs evoke pity, rage, sympathy, anger and frustration, and they travel around the world long before a report on the event has even been conceived. For the most part, they are used to evoke pity, but as the subaltern has demanded more room to speak, the public has been forced to interrogate what we make these images for. Why should black and brown bodies be immortalised in the archives of humanitarianism solely as helpless objects of pity, often devoid of nuance and complexity? What habits do we cultivate in audiences that are fed a steady diet of The Other—hungry, beaten down and helpless?

You can see this debate play out in real time if you scroll through the Instagram accounts of major international humanitarian organisations, for example; you may notice an interesting pattern. For national branch accounts facing the societies where funds are raised—the West and increasingly the Far East—black and brown subjects are photographed either struggling or in the process of receiving assistance. But for accounts facing Africa, Asia and the Middle East—the places where these organisations work—the subjects are often photographed empowered or resolute. In the former, the photographs are a plea for help; in the latter, they offer an appearance of solidarity. Each of these collections tells a specific story about the relationship between the organisation, and who it imagines its audience to be. There's one big unasked question floating through these images: is this how these people see themselves? And if not, is it fair to reduce a person's entire life experience to a single moment for the purposes of raising money?

Perhaps no image captures this controversy like Kevin Carter's *Starving Child and Vulture*. Taken in 1993, the photograph contains two subjects. In the foreground, a young emaciated African child is crouched in a ball with their face to the ground, resting their head on their closed fists. Their ribs are clearly visible, dark skin stretched taut over bone with no muscle or fat in between. In the background on the left, a vulture lurks—as if watching and waiting for the child to die. The grass around the child is parched, and the vulture's dark eyes seem to be alert and ready to pounce.

Starving Child and Vulture raised the alarm on the drought in what is today South Sudan. It fuelled a massive humanitarian response and drove many Western audiences to give to these organisations. But the story behind the story was more complex. According to *Time* magazine, it later emerged that Carter had waited twenty minutes for the vulture to open its wings, in order to capture what he thought was a more powerful photograph. The vulture would not comply, so Carter took his photograph, lit a cigarette and wept. What does that mean—to watch a vulture watching a young child on the brink of death while you wait for the perfect photograph? What does "perfect" mean in this context?

The photograph was later sold to outlets like *The New York Times*. For those who consumed the photograph, it was an important moment for mobilisation, drawing attention to a distant place that they might not otherwise have thought about. Yet the family of the child insisted that they had not abandoned the baby—they had merely put him down while they safely accessed the food distribution. His father said that the child was safer there on the ground than in the melee, where he was likely to be trampled. That part of the story only came to light after people started to interrogate the context of these photographs; only when people began to question what it might mean for South Sudan to be permanently associated with this image. *Starving Child and Vulture* is part of a canon, alongside other iconic photos like *Afghan Girl*—the *National Geographic* cover image of a young girl with striking blue-green eyes—a style of news photography that seems to hit all the right notes with the audiences that consume it, to the detriment of the people it documents.

It turned out that *Starving Child and Vulture* had an effect not only on the photographed, but on the photographer. For Carter, the experience of capturing the image seemed to be part of a broader tapestry of trauma, after years of working to develop the kind of eye that would take this photograph. Four months after he won the Pulitzer Prize for the photograph in 1994, Kevin Carter committed suicide by carbon monoxide poisoning. He was only 33. The young child in the photograph, Kong Nyong, also died, at around age 14 in 2007—perhaps never knowing the impact that his image had had, certainly never profiting from it, and likely never fully comprehending what it meant for him and South Sudan to go into history etched in this way.

Who are we when we only believe in the devastation of the Syrian war when confronted with the picture of a dead child? President Bashar al-Assad has overseen the deaths of more Syrian children than those who have drowned in the Mediterranean Sea—by gassing them, bombing them, and starving them to death. Daesh has killed, kidnapped and orphaned hundreds of children in Syria and Iraq, and those stories are well documented; we have the evidence already that families who leave their homeland do so for self-preservation. Why did this one image of little Alan make all of it so strikingly real, especially for policy-makers? Canada initially denied the Kurdi family refugee status. Europe might have seemed like a possible option, but if they had survived the crossing, they would only have been met with the same troubles as other refugees in Hungary, Macedonia and Serbia. And even if they survived that, they would face the uncertainty of whether the country they had settled in would let them do so indefinitely. The fact that the Kurdis were running away from Syria in clandestine rubber dinghies, instead of being airlifted out, screams volumes about the collapsing refugee protection system, and the hypocrisy of countries that will sell weapons to other states, but deny sanctuary to victims of the wars that then ensue.

* * *

Photographs force us to feel, and to question why we feel the way we do, with an immediacy that words can only aspire to. But photography also walks a fine line between exploitation and empowerment—far more so than writing. The slap-in-the-face experience of looking at a shocking image means that you can't always slow down and digest its full context appropriately. After all, Alan Kurdi's unnecessary death wasn't just about refugees or conflict. It was also about borders, visas, regional integration, and how these man-made structures modify the values around which our societies are built. Kong Nyong's debilitating hunger wasn't just about food being unavailable but about a conflict, sustained in part through international support for the belligerents, choking centuries-old food security systems in one of the world's most arable regions. But this isn't how lay audiences are conditioned to experience photos—especially not humanitarian photos.

We are fed a steady diet of a particular type of suffering, as evidence of Bad Things happening elsewhere in the world. But that also means that we are less likely to believe that the Bad Thing is happening unless the image is made and presented to us. I think this is part of the reason why so many people in the US are having a hard time believing that the coronavirus is real. Having grown accustomed to associating disease outbreaks with images of emaciated black and brown people dying horrible deaths, and having been spared images from US hospitals of people hooked up to ventilators suffering the same, an ordinary person doesn't know how to process the idea of the mass death of white people. There is no mental image they can associate with the startling numbers and frightening speeches, and so they ignore the numbers and the speeches—because they cannot fathom the reality.

This of course isn't an invitation to start mass photography campaigns of sick and dying people. More a realisation that the debate on how to represent suffering in photography goes to the heart of how we organise our societies and our world. It is about the values of empathy and dignity, and the place we accord them in our hierarchies of interests. Images can move action, but that action has consequences; and those making the call as to which images represent which situation need to appreciate this more completely. A photograph of a starving child used to illustrate the story of a war is a direct appeal for intervention, even if it doesn't define what that intervention is. An image of a dead toddler buffeted by the waves of the sea is a critique of a politics that excludes refugees and migrants by any means necessary. The creators of the images scream, "Do something!" and leave it up to us, the consumers, to decide what that something could be.

The tragedy of the Kurdis and the thousands of others who have died in the Mediterranean in the 2010s did something that five years of advocacy by humanitarians had failed to do: it forced a value audit in Europe and beyond. So, while European countries have embraced the idea of a singular European culture that must be preserved at all costs, this value audit has been asking: what about when human lives are at stake? We are in the era of Fortress Europe, shut in against the rest of the world, but is Fortress Europe so sacrosanct an idea that it must be defended even when children are turning up dead? Is there no room in the fortress for empathy?

So should we use more sensational images for humanitarian advocacy, if it brings about this effect? Maybe not, especially when we remember the "CNN effect", whereby continued exposure to macabre images desensitises audiences to such imagery in the long run—which in turn makes the work of raising awareness more difficult. The more audiences have been exposed to pictures of suffering, the more extreme the images have to be to evoke pity. And beyond this consideration is the more important question of the dignity of people photographed in this way. What does it do to individuals and families for the death of their loved one to be turned into a spectacle, particularly when that spectacle is tied to the financial wellbeing of a foreign organisation?

All of this is a question of power, of the power dynamics between photographer, subject and audience, and the gatekeepers standing between them. If we, like the spectator in a gallery, take several steps back and contemplate the tableau, a curious set of second-order questions emerges that complicate the picture even further. Who gets to be a war photographer or a humanitarian photographer? Is it a perfectly even playing field where people from diverse backgrounds get to feed into the practices of image-making and image dissemination? Or is it a world ridden with inequalities that consolidate the dominance of a normative standard determined by a certain eye, a certain perspective, from a certain background? Not everyone can walk into a war zone with an expensive camera and start taking photographs—and not everyone should. Access is necessarily tinged with the biases and vulnerabilities of privilege, or lack thereof. Carter spoke about how he had to bribe soldiers with his cheap watch in order to gain access to the UN feeding programme in Sudan. Not everyone can make those decisions.

With all of these questions around power, race is a factor. Carter was a white South African working in 1993. Even though African wars and crises are where many white Western war photographers come to cut their teeth, African photographers rarely get to do the same; this sets up a dynamic in which African conflicts are fodder to be consumed, to move copy in far-away places. This is changing slowly, and there are notable exceptions—Kenyan photojournalist Mo Amin died one of the highest-profile international photographers. But, for the most part, the war photographer is still a white man who flies in, grabs his image, sells it to a news organisation, and then leaves.

Yet, it would be unfair only to point out the role of the photographer in setting us up to consume the suffering of others in this way. The silent but possibly most influential figure in this power matrix is the photo editor—the person in the newsroom, often far removed from the context in which the photos were taken, who actually makes the decision on what runs with a story and what doesn't. A photographer can take thousands of images in a single trip and only have one published. But if that one photo is published by the right news outlet at the right time, it can—as Carter and other realised—make or break a photographer's career. The news editor never gets a byline and never gets the big prizes, but more than the photographer they decide what our diet of images will be. They are the gatekeepers, but their role is rarely interrogated, leaving photographers like Carter to face the personal consequences.

These questions of power are not abstract theory. We in Kenya have had a direct experience of it, although arguably most Kenyans who witnessed the situation first-hand had no idea what was happening. Over a day and a half in January 2019, the Al Shabaab terror group attacked the Dusit Hotel in Nairobi, gunning down civilians who were working or dining at the upmarket, mixed-use development there. Al Shabaab has been at war with Kenya since 2011, and since the beginning of that conflict, the group has launched numerous assaults on Kenyan territory. But the Dusit attack was one of its most violent and most visible. One of the first photographers on the scene was a Kenyan photographer for the Agence France Presse (AFP), who captured a table in one of the restaurants where four patrons were slouched over their plates, fresh blood oozing out of their bodies onto the pristine white tablecloths and then onto the floor.

The photograph triggered tremendous controversy in Kenya. Like Carter's photograph, it was quickly purchased by *The New York Times* and splashed across their front page. But, unlike Carter's photograph, this one was disseminated in the digital age and the era of social media. As soon as it was published online, the photograph was available in Kenya and subject to thorough criticism from the Kenyan public. As the standoff was still ongoing, there were claims that some people found out that their loved ones had died through that image rather than from the authorities. Unlike the Sudanese people in 1993, the Kenyan public not only had access to the images being taken of them, but also asserted that they did not want to be represented in that way. These are questions of dignity in life and death, and they demanded answers—but the lay audience wasn't sure who direct those demands to.

Kenyans are not the target audience for *The New York Times*, so the paper likely did not consider how they would respond to the packaging of black suffering and black pain for the consumption of Western readers. But many of the nuances of how power shaped the outcome got lost in the opprobrium. For one, the photographer was also Kenyan, and had taken the photo for a newswire, not for *The New York Times*. It didn't help that the *Times* had a reputation for caricatured reporting on the region, nor that the incoming bureau chief took a condescending and defensive line in discussing the images with those who raised their ire. But such is the paradigm of news photography that even when a Kenyan photographer is capturing a Kenyan news event, their work still ends up being used to consume black suffering, rather than empathise with it.

The contours of the debate were a right and justifiable demand for equality before the lens: the bodies of white victims of terror are almost never published in Western newspapers and magazines, even when images are made available by the terror groups themselves, as is the case of Daesh in Syria. Critics rightly point out in such cases that no one should have to find out about the death of a loved one through a front-page or homepage newspaper splash. But the photo editor who has made the decision to purchase such a photograph and put it on the front page never had to deal with the consequences of that decision.

All of this speaks to the culture of news-making that feeds our imagination of what a crisis looks like. Why is it so easy to portray black death in photography in this certain way, even if the person making the image is also raced black? Does the debate change when the creator of the photograph belongs to the community that has criticised its use? It is not enough just to diversify the eyes behind the lens. It's equally important to think about the structural conditions that demand the production of such images: are we so far gone in our hunger for images of suffering as a shortcut to producing empathy that we cannot imagine alternative ways of depicting conflict and human need?

* * *

In the modern era, images of war, suffering and crisis play complicated roles. In international criminal law, for example, photos and footage of war zones that have been shared on social media can provide the basis for open-source investigations of war crimes, and are increasingly part of the tools of international human rights advocacy and litigation. But there is a qualitative difference between the way that kind of image is made and shared, versus images that are made and shared primarily to frighten, or to invite audiences to become spectators in other people's suffering. I think this is what critics of internationally published images like *Starving Child and Vulture* are pushing against. Even at our weakest and most vulnerable, we are more than our suffering, and we deserve the same dignity in our weakness and vulnerability that others—white Westerners—get in theirs.

Photographing crisis should be about more than just consuming the death of the Other. It should be about bearing witness and providing testimony on behalf of those who cannot do so for themselves. The demand for a paradigm shift could come from audiences or from power-holders, but increasing dissatisfaction from audiences especially suggests that the time is nigh. Neither Alan, nor Kong, nor their parents had any say in the way their bodies were used. We deliberately took their images and wove them into our own advocacy narratives without their consent. Of course, anyone could claim that doing so was necessary and ultimately helpful to the broader cause. But that doesn't change underlying facts. There is a palpable unevenness in the way we are able to use the bodies of non-white victims of war and crisis. In the UK, television stations blur or pixellate images of European children in news reports, yet routinely screen advertisements for charitable organisations featuring faces of hungry African or Asian children. What would it look like if we had one standard for image-making, applied to all subjects of all skin colours, and including situations of conflict and crisis?

And until we reach that point, what will the current output do to us as audiences? In the paper "Fear and Loathing in Haiti", Mullings, Werner and Peake have deconstructed the impact of racialised fear (of black people rioting) on the humanitarian response following the 2010 earthquake in Haiti. Heike Härting offers the same critique in relation to a different crisis in the 2008 paper "Global Humanitarianism, Race, and the Spectacle of the African Corpse in Current Western Representations of the Rwandan Genocide". We need to go beyond representations of brown and black death, to question how we represent brown and black experience—in death, in conflicts, at protests, and in other situations where the temptation to tell a preconfigured story is strong.

Images like Alan Kurdi's have impact, and for the most part society has focused on the positive impacts. Before their deaths, he and his brother were just two of the thousands of Syrian children who have died since 2011; of the tens of thousands displaced. Yet it took this photograph, not the volumes of reports on the conflict gathering dust in NGO offices around the world, that pushed people into action: for Canada, which had denied his family regular arrival as a refugee, to give this status to the sole survivor of the disaster, Alan's father. Visual art has a direct line to our empathy centre. It goes there and stays there in a way that words can't. But art alone cannot sustain the weight of dealing with conflict. Eventually the wound scabs back over, and we become less capable of making that human connection. So art as advocacy needs to be used carefully. Shock tactics cannot become the norm.

Nina Simone said in an interview that *Strange Fruit* deals with the ugliness of racial injustice: "ugly in the sense that it ... tears at the guts of what white people have done to my people in this country." Similarly, Demir's photograph of little Alan and Galip deals with the ugliness of war. It tears at the guts of collective apathy. It reminds us that war happens to people—that behind every statistic is a name, a face and a family. But I don't think we should need photographs of dead infants to be reminded of this. Instead we probably need to spend more time unpacking why we needed a thousand words before we could empathise with other people's suffering.

4

THE END OF ASYLUM

By 2019, a small tent city was taking shape in Tapachula, on the Mexico–Guatemala border. Its inhabitants were and are living proof of the systematic erosion of a foundational principle of the post-World War II international order. The residents are primarily refugees and migrants from African countries who have fled political persecution, social upheaval and economic uncertainty, taking one of the longest and most perilous migration routes in the world in the hope of reaching the United States.

Until September 2019, most would have been granted a twenty-one-day grace period to either normalise their residency status in Mexico or continue on to the US border. But in that month, the US Supreme Court ruled that the administration of President Donald Trump can deny asylum to anyone who has crossed a third country en route to the US border. As a result, Mexico started denying Africans free passage through its territory. And so the migrants arriving in Tapachula have nowhere to go. They are trapped between hardline US asylum policies, Mexico's acquiescence to those policies, and a growing global backlash against anyone seeking asylum.

TRAVELLING WHILE BLACK

The United States is far from the only country to have slammed its gates on those fleeing crumbling social, political and economic systems. Around the world, rich and poor countries alike are pulling up their drawbridges, slashing the number of refugees they are willing to accept, and denying asylum to those who might have been admitted in the past. Europe, for instance, sunk to a new low in the summer of 2019 by criminalising rescue in the Mediterranean, allowing preventable deaths at sea, and forcibly returning vulnerable people to torture and indefinite detention in Libya.

In Africa, Asia, and South America, the mood is much the same. Kenya is building a wall along its border with Somalia and sending thousands of Somali refugees back into a war zone. Bangladesh plans to repatriate thousands of Rohingya refugees to Myanmar with the help of the UN Refugee Agency, despite other UN agencies warning that returnees still face the threat of genocide. Across South America and the Caribbean, Venezuelans fleeing their country's economic collapse have been met with sudden policy changes designed to make them ineligible for asylum, while Australia's extraterritorial detention system, based on the Pacific island of Nauru, remains a symbol of the violent lengths to which that country is willing to go to prevent people from seeking safety from within its borders.

Demand for asylum has never been higher, and in 2019 for example there were 25.9 million people around the world fleeing their countries as a result of war and instability. Yet the list of countries willing to take them in is shrinking by the day, as the international system that created the right to asylum and is bound to protect it becomes increasingly complicit in its demise. If there were a theme song to 2019, it would have been a dirge for the end of safe harbour.

* * *

Derived from the ancient Greek *asulos*, which roughly translates to "inviolable", the word asylum first entered the English lexicon in the late Middle Ages, when it was understood to mean "an inviolable shelter or protection from pursuit or arrest". By definition, an asylum-seeker was a person who sought a form of protection that could never be violated, broken or infringed. Throughout history, various nations have recognised or aspired to some version of the right to asylum—from the ancient Greek and Hebrew civilisations, to medieval England and the French First Republic. In Europe, the history of asylum is closely intertwined with that of religious discrimination and strife. When the Catholic monarchs of Spain ordered the expulsion of hundreds of thousands of Jews in 1492, for example, many sought refuge in Turkey, Italy and North Africa. Many of the atrocities of World War II were in fact the culmination of violent and discriminatory practices that had caused episodic displacement for centuries. One major distinction between these previous eras and the Nazi period, however, was that targeted groups, including Jews, Roma, Sinti and gay people, saw their avenues of escape gradually closed off. Between 1933 and 1945, there was little willingness in the "international community" to take them in.

In 1938, representatives of thirty-two countries met in Evian, France to try to agree on a coordinated response to the refugee crisis in Europe. While all recognised the gravity of the situation, most nations steadfastly refused to accept more refugees. Thus, in 1939, most of the over 900 Jews fleeing Nazi persecution on board the *S.S. St Louis* were turned away by Cuba; the ship was also refused permission to dock in the United States and finally Canada, before it returned to Europe, where the Nazis eventually executed 254 of the passengers.

This shameful history explains the centrality of the principle of asylum to the post-war world order. Its inviolability was seen as necessary to stop Europe's endless cycle of war and displacement. The Universal Declaration of Human Rights, adopted by the UN

General Assembly in 1948, declared that "Everyone has the right to seek and to enjoy in other countries asylum from persecution." The 1951 Convention Relating to the Status of Refugees, also known as the Geneva Convention, codified this protection for anyone persecuted on the basis of race, religion, nationality, political opinion, or membership of a particular social group. However, the Convention detailed the right of asylum-seekers to *seek* asylum—it was far more vague on the right to have it granted.

As a result, asylum became an ad hoc and often political affair. During the Cold War, both the United States and the Soviet Union almost always granted asylum to political dissidents from the other side, while also extending permissive immigration policies to countries in their spheres of influence. In much of the rest of the world, asylum was handled on a situational basis—again, often to serve explicitly political ends. For example, people fleeing apartheid in Zimbabwe and South Africa routinely received protection, legal status and travel documents from other African countries looking to contribute to the broader anti-apartheid struggle.

After the end of the Cold War, world powers had less interest and fewer opportunities to instrumentalise asylum politically, and refugee protection became more formalised as a legal and bureaucratic practice. At the same time, however, civil conflicts in places like Somalia, Angola and the former Yugoslavia produced extended turmoil and millions of refugees. As pressure mounted on receiving countries, many decided that these refugees did not meet the rigid, bureaucratic requirements of the 1951 Refugee Convention: fear of general violence or instability did not fit neatly into any of the five narrow categories of persecution outlined in the UN text. When millions needed asylum the most, countries defined the right to it as narrowly as they could, so as to shoulder the least possible burden.

* * *

Thus began the age of encampment. Around the world, countries receiving large numbers of refugees began to force the displaced into camps. Usually, the host governments granted these new arrivals prima facie refugee status, because they had fled their home countries en masse, but rarely did they go through the process of adjudicating individual asylum claims. As a result, these people were often treated as second-class refugees, unable to access the same rights and freedoms as refugees granted asylum through an individual determination process or resettled to a third country like the United States or Canada. Many were denied freedom of movement, barred from receiving international travel documents, and given limited access to education and healthcare outside the camp.

The scale of displacement after the end of the Cold War quickly overwhelmed major host countries like Kenya and Pakistan, as well as the UN system that kept the camps running. People with prima facie recognition but not full refugee status remained in limbo for decades. Some countries tightened the bureaucratic standards for full status even further, and many applications stalled indefinitely. Even then, the host countries insisted that the camps be treated as temporary, a designation that made the denial of full refugee status more politically palatable.

The alarming rise in encampment—and the realisation that the camps were anything but temporary—should have catalysed a review of the 1951 Convention, with the aim of closing the gap between refugees with full status and those who remained in camps. Instead, the international community responded with a measure of delusion, refusing to recognise that the camps were slowly becoming permanent open-air prisons. To agree on a new convention at a time when more and more countries wanted less and less asylum would no doubt have been difficult. Already, the guiding philosophy in many countries had shifted from default inclusion to default exclusion. But failure to end this two-tiered system—in which some refugees enjoy the full protections of the Convention while others remain perpetual asylum-seekers at the mercy of host governments—set the stage for the current crisis.

That most of the countries hosting large numbers of asylum-seekers were poor countries, while rich countries led the way in eroding the right to asylum, was no accident. UN agencies, whose budgets are mainly funded by rich countries, are complicit in maintaining this status quo. Some asylum-seekers have eventually been resettled from the camps to third countries, mainly in the developed world, but only a tiny fraction of those in need of asylum. And so the camps have become permanent cities. Today, there are millions of people around the world who have never known life outside of a refugee camp. The Dadaab complex in Kenya, for example, was until recently the largest refugee camp in the world, with a population of more than 500,000. But Dadaab doesn't exist on official maps of Kenya, even though at its peak it would have been the country's third largest city. Its residents enjoy none of the rights of Kenyan citizenship. A third generation of Somali refugees has been born in Dadaab, with almost no hope of citizenship in Kenya, no reason to return to Somalia and no reasonable expectation of being resettled elsewhere.

Today the status of asylum as an international legal principle is more tenuous than ever. The age of encampment has led to an intensifying global retrenchment, as the poor countries bearing the brunt of the burden are now also reluctant to accept more asylum-seekers. Some, with the co-operation of the United Nations, are actively returning refugees to conflict zones, in clear breach of the 1951 Convention.

At the same time, crises not contemplated at the time of the Convention expose the regime's inadequacy. Large-scale commercial logging has displaced whole Indigenous communities from the rainforests of Brazil and Indonesia. Rising sea levels threaten island nations and coastal cities whose residents could soon be uprooted. And higher global temperatures will eventually make parts of the world uninhabitable while fuelling extreme weather events like Hurricane Dorian, which levelled much of the Bahamas earlier in mid-2019. Yet there is no internationally recognised definition of a climate refugee, no doubt because many countries remain slow to appreciate the threat.

In an ideal world, now would be the time to review and update the 1951 Refugee Convention. That was the original goal of many who pushed for the Global Compact for Refugees, a new international framework for addressing the refugee crisis, which the UN General Assembly passed at the end of 2018. But this non-binding framework fell far short of expectations, failing to sufficiently shift the responsibility for hosting refugees from poor to rich countries, and doing nothing to expand or even defend the right to asylum. Viktor Orbán's Hungary and the United States stood alone and voted against the Compact, limited and toothless though it was.

Both of the ideas embedded in the historical definition of asylum—inviolability and protection—are under attack as never before. Soon after her appointment as head of the European Commission in 2019, Ursula von der Leyen changed the title of her migration commissioner to "vice president for protecting our European way of life", seemingly endorsing the idea that migration is a threat to Europe. There was a brief moment of social media outrage, but the discourse around refugees in Europe remains unchanged. Few political leaders anywhere in the world are willing to defend the inviolability of the right to asylum. And this is how asylum will end—in a low boil of ambivalence that will eventually consume this foundational principle of our existing political system.

5

THE SEA THAT EATS OUR CHILDREN

Sometime in April 2017, I looked up and looked around and realised where I was. Another conference in another part of the world, talking about being part of the solution in jargon and abstraction. Words that flowed so easily and perfectly, but were slowly starting to lose their meaning because they were so disconnected from the work they claimed to do in the world. Empowerment. Multi-stakeholder. Even protection. I don't know if the people at the meeting could tell, but I found myself testing the flavour of the words in my mouth and finding them indistinct and flavourless, like jello or cotton candy—two foods that taste of nothing and do nothing. Just meaningless carbohydrates.

I bought a ticket on a whim. A last-minute decision to try and recover a sense of purpose after growing increasingly jaded with the journey my professional life was on. Like most people, I had read all the headlines and I knew all the stories, but I couldn't explain to you exactly why these stories—of young men and women crowded in rubber dinghies and crashing against each other as the waves of the sea rose and fell around them—made me want to get on the move. I wanted to do something more;

61

but I wasn't finding it particularly easy to figure out what that meant. Heaven knows, I could barely afford the flight. And I really should have been resting after travelling so much already that month. But I wanted to be useful, so I listened to my spirit when it said, "Go and witness."

What I was off to witness was one of the most urgent humanitarian crises of the twenty-first century. The Mediterranean Sea is only 2,400 miles across, or about half the length of continental Africa, but in the 2010s it earned distinction as the largest mass burial site for Africans in the modern world. Although crossings between Africa, Asia and Europe are as old as settlement along its shores, in the modern era, restrictions on travel and violent border security have turned the sea into a mass graveyard, where countries would rather return vulnerable people to death or near-certain slavery than allow for a measure of safety. Almost all of Europe is complicit in turning people away at their most vulnerable, including by intimidating boats defying the fortress that Europe built.

The sea is unpredictable—from above, it glimmers and undulates rhythmically to create a false sense of predictability. But it is a cruelly variable place, and at any moment those rhythmic undulations can crescendo into violent waves that upturn flimsy boats and suck even the strongest bodies under. For about three years between 2016 and 2019, it felt like another dinghy was overturning every day or every few hours. Another group of people dying.

I fly from Rome to Palermo, the largest city on the island of Sicily, and I don't really have a plan. I've been trying to establish myself as a human rights lawyer for three years by this time, and in the course of my work I've encountered primarily Europeans and Americans. Some time around the turn of the millennium, there developed an unspoken consensus that humanitarian work at the policy-making level was for white people, and brown and black people were to be talked about. They might contribute with the most menial tasks, but they were never in the room for conversations about what to do next.

THE SEA THAT EATS OUR CHILDREN

This thing that I'm doing in going to Palermo is not a thing that Africans generally do. White people do this. They buy the ticket and figure out the purpose when they get there. Often they slot into pre-existing communities that will make the transition easier—someone with a room to rent, someone else with a car they can borrow, someone who might be able to offer some paid work. This, I think, is what it means to be an expatriate—to have these pre-configured networks of access and privilege that take the sting out of the dislocation and disorientation of entering a new society as a rank outsider. We who are black and travelling without these preconfigured structures of support and acceptance, we don't get to be expats—we are migrants, refugees or just Other.

So there's a part of me that is desperately curious to find out if this goes for black people in Europe too. Until now, every time I have gone to Europe, I have had to announce to the government in question every step of my travel, in advance. But between a week of meetings in Geneva, a week of meetings and workshops in South Africa and a return to Brussels, I have a visa window: a brief period of time when I have a valid Schengen visa that gives me permission to travel throughout Europe somewhat freely. So instead of going home I decide to buy a ticket from Geneva to Rome, and then Rome to Palermo—to see what I can access when showing up this way. Can I find my way up close to the fracture lines that I've been reading about?

April is around the time when winter in the Mediterranean is thawing, but spring has not yet sprung, and the climate around the sea is a little favourable for even the smaller boats. But it is 2017, a crisis year, and so the boats are arriving at record rates. The law of the sea prohibits one vessel from abandoning another in distress on the open water, and European governments have not yet put in place the inhumane rules that will stop rescue boats from docking in their ports at the end of the decade. So, day after day, boats will arrive in Palermo, packed to the rafters with people—mostly young, and mostly male—who have spent weeks or even years walking and then swimming towards something that those of us with a regular roof over our heads and food on the table might never fully understand. Huge commercial tankers with hundreds of weather-worn people leaning over the side, often wide-eyed, terrified and traumatised. Small rescue ships commissioned by international non-profits that ignore government directives to let people die.

And these are the lucky ones. In the twenty-first century, the Mediterranean has devoured thousands of people who have become victims not of the sea as such, but of increasing hostility to outsiders around the world, and of the way that European inclusion policy and Western politics of policing have expanded to this part of the water. Certainly, more Africans have died of other causes, but nowhere else are more African civilians buried together. In 2016, 3,784 deaths were recorded in the Mediterranean Sea. Many were Africans, but attention to the waters only grew after a spike in arrivals from Syria and the Levant—victims of wars funded by Western and regional politics. It used to be that the most tenacious walked all the way from Bangladesh, across Asia and Africa; but since conditions across Libya deteriorated in the early 2010s, that has slowly been shifting. Now, as the war rages around them, we notice the scars of people who survive the horrors of detention camps in Libya, funded by European governments to keep the Other out. Between 2016 and 2019, at least 17,000 people will die attempting that crossing, many because European governments in the countries on the Mediterranean have put in place policies arguing that migration is the single biggest existential threat to European identity.

* * *

THE SEA THAT EATS OUR CHILDREN

The deaths on the Mediterranean Sea have wrongly been framed as an African, a Syrian or even a Libyan crisis; as being about migration. While Europe has been quick to hijack the discussion and declare this a crisis of the European border, in fact it's a crisis of the European state—one that has everything to do with the history of conflict and division within that continent. So much of how the world's states function and fear comes from Europe's bloody and violent history. Take sovereignty, a principle defined by the peace of Westphalia in 1648, which ended a war that had killed about 8 million people. We may take the concept of Westphalian sovereignty as today's default for international political organisation, but it was born out of the European history of conquest and mutual destruction. Even in Europe itself, it didn't lead to lasting peace until the end of the twentieth century, with the last two major conflicts—in Bosnia and Northern Ireland—only coming to a close in the mid-1990s. And now, those hard-won presumptions about the role of the state in international life are being challenged. What does equality before the law mean in multi-ethnic societies? How can strong borders coexist with humanitarian protection? How can countries preach principles in other parts of the world while ignoring those principles at home, yet still aspire to some form of global leadership?

When I was an undergrad, I found that reading Immanuel Wallerstein's world-systems theory, developed in the 1970s, helped me get a grip on how a border can become an object of export. Dividing the world into countries of the core and countries of the periphery, Wallerstein said that countries of the periphery are primarily former colonies or dependencies, incorporated into the world economy only in line with their capacity to provide raw materials to the countries of the core, which turn them into manufactured goods. The peripheral country is not imagined as a complex place with variable history and dynamics;

yet the core country, despite being defined by its consumption, *is* endowed with political nuance.

Even after the age of empires, the latter half of the twentieth century is remembered particularly for its proxy wars. Ethiopia and Somalia destroyed each other for the sake of Cold War interests, for example. Leaders like Mobutu Sese Seko destroyed their own populations in the name of capitalism. Today, money may have replaced ideology as the driving force of the proxy war, but countries of the core still manufacture weapons that are sold to countries of the periphery, in order to sustain chaos and conflict that allows for depressed prices on raw materials. War is one of the most consistently profitable industries in the modern world, and much of Europe's peace and prosperity has come at the expense of peace in other parts of the world, particularly through sales of arms to poor countries that should ideally be spending that money on something else. Powerful countries will side with whoever guarantees the most access to resources. In the end, this means that countries of the core are fighting wars indirectly, through military co-operation arrangements and financial support for various factions or entities in regional wars far away. The war in Syria is framed as a conflict between the government and dissidents, but not as a conflict between the various governments that continue to sell weapons to both sides.

The only thing that could challenge the world order of arms sales from core to periphery would be citizens of the core asking difficult questions about where the money comes from—but technology has made it possible to insulate civilians from the political consequences of decisions governments take in their name. Drones, for example, make it seem like the US military— the largest and best-resourced in the world—is pursuing a more humanitarian approach to conflict. But in fact what it is doing is shifting all the risks of conflict to one side. The US soldier sends a drone to Somalia or Afghanistan to kill a family of twenty-one without ever having to take any personal risk—sometimes without out even having to leave home. But what does it do to soldiers when entire societies are removed from the consequences of their actions? What does it mean when citizens can fund wars through their taxes, without having to deal with the reality of what war is and what it does?

It makes people cruel. Making war abstract in this way dehumanises it. In *Homage to Catalonia*, George Orwell writes eloquently about the futility and wastefulness of war. The reality of being a soldier is endless hours of idle waiting, the risk of getting shot by your own side, and facing a strange, solitary death. Modern warfare has only made this wastefulness more extreme. People who never have to go through this bizarre, traumatic experience can vote in favour of war in places that they can't even identify on a map. No one thinks of the victims or collateral damage on the other side. It becomes almost like a video game where everything is an abstract hypothetical; except it's not. War is sending people out to cause harm and to kill other people. Regardless of how the decision to go to war is framed, people should know what they are getting into.

Over time, war has become shrouded in jargon and evasive methods—to paraphrase what Orwell once said, we have used political language to give an aura of civility to inhumane behaviour. Not victims, but targets. Instead of ending war, we're getting better at talking around it, and as a consequence we are becoming less connected to the reality of what war is. Most of us no longer understand what it means to live in a war, to survive a war or to be made a refugee by war, because we are never confronted with the reality of what war does. We—and especially those of us who make our living by analysing politics—talk about it as if it's an elaborate, well-thought-out chess game, when in fact it is a clumsy, only slightly elevated game of Ludo. War is chaos, upheaval and futility. So we've focused on making it harder and harder for ordinary people to look at and see it, eroding our capacity for empathy and hospitality toward the people running away.

I think in some ways this is why I went to Palermo. I could feel myself becoming insulated from the reality of what I hoped I was doing. Everything was becoming shrouded in legalese and I had, despite my efforts, become a bureaucrat whose primary role was fundraising. I felt myself losing sight of what I was fighting for on a fundamental, human level. I was uncomfortable with the way I was consuming news about events. In my work, I felt like I was being pushed more and more to look away from the harm caused by so many personal and public decisions around this issue—to take the narratives and operationalise them for fundraising, but never to really sit in the discomfort of the world we were building. I didn't go to Palermo just to be a voyeur, consuming other people's suffering for spectacle or second-degree horror. I wanted to be useful; but to do that properly, I had to understand what I was talking about. I had to see.

* * *

There are three main routes that will get you across the Mediterranean from Africa or Asia into Europe. The Western route runs from Morocco and the Spanish enclave of Ceuta, across to Spain and Portugal. At its narrowest, the Strait of Gibraltar that separates Spain from Morocco is only 9 miles across—you can actually see Europe from the Moroccan coastline—but the water is choppy and unpredictable, because this is the place where the warm Mediterranean Sea meets the cold Atlantic Ocean. The Eastern route runs from Egypt to Turkey and Greece; it is mostly used by refugees from the Middle East, but also Somali and Eritrean people, who might alternatively cross into Yemen via Djibouti before heading across the Persian Gulf. The central route runs from Libya to Italy, today taking people from the violence and trauma of Libya into the political uncertainty and rising nationalism of Italy.

These routes have been used for almost as long as travel across the Mediterranean has been documented. Scattered across the coastline is the detritus of ancient civilisations that fed into the birth of the modern age—Sparta in Greece, Carthage in Tunisia, Alexandria in Egypt, historical Athens and Rome—telling a story of societies that have been in constant if not always friendly contact with each other. If Western philosophy is a cornerstone of Western politics and society, it's worth noting that many of the most notable products of Western philosophy are in fact products of the free movement of people and ideas across the water. Augustine of Hippo was an African man whose theology and philosophy are at the heart of modern Christianity and Western political thought. His theory of the just war is still taught in international relations and political science classes all around the world. Historians say that Augustine was Berber— from a pastoralist people—and so migration and mobility was central to his worldview even before he moved to Rome and Milan to continue his work. Movement has always been central to the Mediterranean region's intellectual fertility, and modern hostility to it is only contributing to its decline.

It's not that there has never before been hostility between the communities of the Mediterranean. Remember: Europe has always been a violent place. But as Europe has coalesced into an enormous social and political project, the scope of the damage has become greater. Bertrand Russell once wrote that leaders have always been stupid, but they have never been quite so pow-erful before; he was writing of the period between the world wars, but the same can be said today. The human capacity to inflict harm is greater than it has ever been, which makes histori-cal tensions and hatreds all the more dangerous. Alarming num-bers of people are now dying while using routes that have been in place for hundreds of years.

TRAVELLING WHILE BLACK

After the end of the Cold War in 1989, as European countries turned their full attention to consolidating around the European Union, they looked to harmonise immigration policies between countries with very different historical attitudes to migration and integration. On the one hand were countries like Italy, which hadn't coalesced into a single state until late in the nineteenth century and which had a long history of both emigration and immigration; on the other were small citadels like Luxembourg, surrounded by mountains that had long excluded outsiders, and preferring a certain cultural monotony.

The 1990 Schengen Convention found a way to keep both the historically open and the historically closed countries happy, despite the new system abolishing internal visa controls and agreeing common visa policies (to reduce bureaucracy at many European countries' borders). The compromise was an invasive, humiliating and even violent process of scrutiny for people coming from countries considered to be too poor, and thus a risk for immigration.

Humanitarians will tell you that one thing the Schengen system did with alarming efficiency was to close off all humane routes into Europe for citizens of these unwanted countries who could not meet the required thresholds. For a young man or woman from Senegal or Sudan who couldn't find work in a village ravaged by climate change, or a collapsing economy, the Schengen regime left no legal way to seek low-wage work in Europe. Of course it was not ideal that people had been boarding flights to Europe and then claiming asylum or overstaying their tourist visas. But at least they'd been arriving alive. What the architects of Schengen seemed to ignore was the sheer number of people who would now be driven towards smugglers and clandestine routes instead. When people see their options as certain death while standing still, versus a minute chance of success if they move, they will move.

THE SEA THAT EATS OUR CHILDREN

Whenever I make this argument to Europeans, I always get a version of "So why don't the people in those countries just take charge of their politics and make their countries better?" Of course that would be the better and even the ideal option. But go back to Wallerstein and the use of borders to export instability out of the West. Look at the twentieth century in Africa alone. First the violence of colonisation and invasion. Then the widespread, targeted assassination, with the collaboration of Western governments, of visionary leaders like Thomas Sankara and Patrice Lumumba. Then decades of active economic interference and sabotage, culminating in the Structural Adjustment Programs of the late 1980s: loans from the IMF and World Bank to economies in crisis, on condition of structural reforms. Now, we have digital colonialism and Western governments providing cover for private Western corporations to interfere in the politics of developing countries. Do you still think it's fair to place responsibility on civilians for choices made by states? Why don't the countries manufacturing and selling weapons to poorer governments just stop doing it? Why don't governments just stop supporting dictators? Emigration doesn't happen in a vacuum.

The number of people taking to the seas to get to Europe hasn't just been increasing because there are simply more people. It's because legal and safe passage to Europe has disappeared, for all but a small sliver of the world's population. For most of the 2000s, while the world's economy was flourishing, European countries were content to look the other way as these clandestine routes also flourished. But as things took a turn after the 2007–8 global financial crash, politicians in many European countries required a quick win, and with the Schengen settlement already in place, migrants and refugees—particularly people who stood out because of their race—were a soft target.

Even so the story of how Europe turned on undocumented migrants in the 2000s would be incomplete without a quick

71

detour into African politics, and specifically the death of Muammar Gaddafi. Colonel Gaddafi seized power in Libya in 1961 and, until his death in 2011, proved a master in pitting different regional powers against each other in order to serve his political agenda. To some people, Gaddafi remains a hero, particularly for his bold criticisms of European geopolitical manipulation in Africa. He funded a great deal of infrastructure in countries like Uganda and Burkina Faso, and although his early pan-Arab efforts failed, he was the driving force behind the African Union, overseeing its transformation into a formidable geopolitical player and reigniting Kwame Nkrumah's vision of eliminating borders in Africa—just as white countries were doing in Europe. He welcomed people from sub-Saharan Africa to Libya and provided them with opportunities to work—so long as they remained loyal to him.

But Gaddafi also sowed the seeds for widespread violence and disruption, by training hundreds of thousands of militias ostensibly resisting European expansionism across the Sahel. At home in Libya, the colonel was violent and cruel with his own citizens, driving thousands into exile and hanging students, lawyers and other dissidents in public squares—even redirecting traffic in town so that everyone would have to drive past the bodies. After the 1988 bombing that crashed Pan Am Flight 103 over the Scottish town of Lockerbie, Gaddafi denied the American and British claim that he was behind the attack, and largely refused to co-operate with investigations or prosecutions despite sanctions and military interventions from both countries—accepting responsibility and paying reparations to the victims only in 2003, after oil prices had declined.

Gaddafi's regime and the developing regime of European integration were always intertwined. One of the ways he managed to keep open channels of communication and extort concessions from the European Union—even during Libya's years under sanction—was through Europe's fear of African mobility. This anti-black border policy gave Gaddafi tremendous leverage, because Europe was boxed in by its own appeals to humanitarianism and human rights as a core political doctrine of the EU project. At the same time as actively intervening to provide search and rescue for distressed boats, Europe was relying on Libyan government intervention to hold back African people wanting to cross. At one conference, Gaddafi allegedly tried to elicit more funding from the EU by threatening to send so many Africans to Europe that it would "turn black".

Thus Gaddafi had for many years been the custodian of the central route across the Mediterranean, and his border policy the main determining factor in the number of people using the route to get to Europe. Then came the so-called Arab Spring in 2011. The protest movement began in neighbouring Tunisia, but when the Tunisian president fled, his ousting inspired a wave of similar uprisings across the Middle East and North Africa. Despite regime attempts to placate society, protests in Libya escalated and culminated in a civil war during which the colonel was assassinated by his own former soldiers in October 2011.

When Gaddafi was toppled, Libya—a state built around an individual wielding near-absolute power—fell apart. Suddenly there were new opportunities for all kinds of political mercenaries, and Europe could no longer exercise extraterritorial control over Libya's migration policy: hundreds of thousands of people from the Sahel, but also from as far afield as Bangladesh, began exploiting the political vacuum to attempt the crossing. The central route quickly overtook the Western route as the preferred access point across the sea.

In 2014, Italy launched a project called Operation Mare Nostrum—Latin for "our sea" and an affectionate term for the Mediterranean dating to ancient Roman times. Between 2013 and 2014, as numbers of people taking to the waters rose, the

Italian navy actively rescued an estimated 150,000 people from boats in distress. The European Commission provided initial funding for the project, but for Italy it became expensive and unsustainable. Only Slovenia provided an additional boat for the project, which the Italian government claimed cost it approximately €114 million. Rome ended the humanitarian mission after it was unable to secure more financial and material support, and it was replaced by European border security and surveillance projects with only a small commitment to search and rescue— Operation Triton, which ran until 2018, and now Operation Themis. The criminalisation of migration across the central route was complete, and this was the new way that Europe was going to enforce it.

After co-ordinated humanitarian efforts ceased in 2014, the central route became the most deadly way across the Mediterranean. Between 2014 and 2015, the number of people dying along the route increased ten times over. By the time I arrived in Palermo in April 2017, 1,002 deaths had been recorded so far that year in the straits between Libya and Tunisia, a 17.5% increase on the previous year. To put this in context, if it were a war zone, the Mediterranean Sea would have been the most violent conflict in Africa in 2017. As numbers rose, so did European hostility to these arrivals, and some European governments threatened to prosecute humanitarian agencies for intervening to save those left stranded on the high seas.

The peak of deaths in the mid-2010s may now have passed, but Europe's divisions on migration have not gone away. In 2019, Captain Carola Rackete of the *Sea-Watch 3* was arrested by Italian officials for ignoring an Italian blockade on rescue ships and delivering forty people it had picked up to Lampedusa. The then Italian foreign minister, Matteo Salvini, accused her of threatening an Italian ship and undermining European law. Rackete, a German sea captain with a Masters degree in conservation from a

British university, was sailing under a Dutch flag with a predomi-
nantly German crew. In her native Germany, over €1 million was
crowd-funded for her defence. In the Netherlands, the two main
parties of the governing coalition issued a statement castigating
her and other NGOs for running "a ferry service" for migrants
and refugees. The city of Paris offered her their highest honour,
which Rackete declined, to protest the Italian and Maltese
embargoes. Europe is sharply divided on what its policy in the
Mediterranean should be. If there is a crisis of migration in the
Mediterranean it is not in Africa. It is in Europe. This is a crisis
of a structure struggling to reconcile its illusions about what it is
with the reality of what it does.

* * *

Bertrand Russell put it this way in his essay *Western Civilisa-
tion*: "I am afraid Europe, however intelligent, has always been
rather horrid, except in the brief period between 1848 and
1914. Now, unfortunately, Europeans are reverting to type."
Russell wrote these words between the world wars, but his
words remain prescient today, particularly with regards to
human mobility and despite the horrifying statistics of deaths
at sea. Most of those making the crossing from Libya are
young single men—people targeted for forced conscription by
militaries and militias at home, but the focus of many white
Western fears about immigration and foreigners. Many of them
come from countries that are not instantly associated with conflict. Nigeria and Somalia are clear exceptions, but a number of
the arrivals come from the Gambia, Senegal, Sierra Leone,
Eritrea and beyond the African continent.

I went to Palermo, the capital of Sicily, where hundreds of
young Africans arrive each week, because I wanted to understand
the difference between young people who leave and those like
me who remain. The vast majority of what is written about the

ongoing crisis is written with the idea that African migration is a problem for Europe to solve. This is partially true, in the sense that European countries have created the impetus for much of this migration, with their tacit support for African autocracies in places like the Gambia, their financing and arming of conflicts in places like Libya, and their toxic economic policies in countries like Niger. But that is a moral emergency, not a practical one. In practical terms, the 1.015 million migrants who made the European crossing in 2017 are only an intimidating number if you ignore the fact that a similar number of Syrian refugees currently live in Lebanon alone.

The idea of the Mediterranean crisis as a European crisis has never quite sat right with me, given that the vast majority of those losing their lives are African or Middle Eastern. I went to Palermo because I wanted to recentre, even for myself, African voices in a conversation about so many young Africans dying anonymous deaths on the high seas. I wanted to know if the experience of a violent crossing—and staring down the prospect of an untimely underwater death—had changed their perspectives of their home countries and of the reasons why they left. I wanted to know if living in Europe had changed their minds about leaving Africa.

I was not really afraid of Palermo until I got out of the airport. After the first twenty or thirty, an airport is just an airport, except maybe the really small, unusual ones where things can get out of control very quickly if you drop your attention. But once you leave the airport, the reality of a place and the enormity of the decision you've taken can hit you like a tonne of bricks. Suddenly, when I leave the airport and I need to take a taxi, I remember that I don't speak a word of Italian. All the stories I've heard of racism and intimidation of people who look like me zip from the back of my mind to the front, crowding out much of the rational thought. But I know quickly what needs to happen next—one foot in front of the other. Get to the Airbnb, get something to eat, sleep off the anxiety.

Palermo is not what I expected. I thought it would be beautiful, and it is: the architecture is breathtaking and as richly diverse as Sicily's history. But the vibe isn't at all what I had been prepared for. Instead of a city ossified in anger and hatred, I find a community struggling to understand and honestly engage with its position in a complex historical moment, where Sicilians are living with the reality of decisions taken thousands of kilometres away in Rome or Brussels. There is no single narrative of how Palermo feels about migration, but the city is built on a legacy of migration and economic marginalisation, one that it faces every day. No one seems surprised to see me there—a couple of curious glances, but for the most part I am ignored. On the whole, I don't sense any of the overt hostility I've detected in many other cities in Europe. I get more reactions in New York's Upper East Side than I'm getting in Palermo's wide streets.

On that first day, I stumble upon three ongoing cultural installations that testify to Palermo's complexity. The Arab-Norman Palermo trail, supported by UNESCO, guides the visitor to the relics of twelfth-century Arab migration to Sicily—churches with minaret-shaped steeples that were repurposed by the Catholic Church from the Islamic communities that built them. An exhibition by Enzo Venezia at the Museum of Contemporary art, titled *A.C.I.D.O.*, includes a massive installation called *Caronte*, a nod to the memory and trauma of shipwreck that features pictures of migrants from all over the world and of Italian art submerged in a metaphorical sea. The Cappella dell'Incoronazione museum hosts *No Borders*, featuring art from Iran, Iraq, Libya, Syria, Somalia, Sudan and Yemen, directly confronting the US ban on arrivals from these countries. If the art is anything to go by, Palermitanos at least have the advantage of being interested in a humane, nuanced conversation about what migration and mobility means to this unique island. Which is good, because the island and the city are at the centre of Italy and Europe's experience of African migration.

The next day, I do nothing but walk the streets to get a sense of the town, but at the end of it I'm still struggling. I head down to the water and walk along the marina, but it is mostly cruise ships and closed storefronts, so I loop back to take in some of the town. But when I catch up with one of my contacts later that afternoon, I learn about the boat that's coming in the next morning.

This is how I encounter my first group of Africans in Palermo. The contact has told me that a boat is arriving at the docks at 8 a.m. the following day, and I make plans to be there when it does. It is a commercial boat, but because there are cruise ships docking at the same time, the docks will be more or less open to the public, just with an intensive security presence. So I head down and wait. At first I am the only person there not affiliated with the humanitarian organisations that have set up assistance tents along the docks. Then one or two people with cameras and notepads begin trickling in, followed by men and women in all kinds of uniforms, until eventually there's a sizeable crowd. At one point, we are all looking at the horizon, where a small smudge in the distance inches closer and closer, one painful second after another, until it finally comes into full view. A gigantic cargo ship teeming with people looking ambivalently over its edge, all quietly watching us watching them.

I don't think I've ever really thought before about how big a cargo ship could be. This tanker is almost four or five storeys high. By the time it docks fully, I have to crane my neck at an obtuse angle to keep sight of the people aboard the *Tuna I*. The boat is docking in Palermo with 470 rescued migrants and refugees aboard, adding to the 8,360 people saved from fifty-five distressed dinghies on the central route during the Easter week-end just gone. For the next two hours we stand witness to a haunting ritual. First some officials from the local Red Cross, accompanied by local security, board the ship to give instructions. We can't hear what is said on board because the *Tuna I* is so massive, though it rocks lightly with the waves.

After a few minutes, the procession begins, the heavy clunking of bare feet colliding harshly with the metal of the boat's steps. Every person who disembarks is forced to leave their shoes on board, so they stumble down the stairs, grabbing hold of either the railing or whatever meagre possessions they still have on their person. Each one gets their moment on the steps: at no point are two people allowed to disembark at the same time. The vast majority of those rescued are black men with dark skin like mine, whose curly hair has turned coppery brown at the tips—perhaps from sunlight, but more likely from malnutrition. There are also a handful of Bangladeshis and East Africans (Eritrean or Ethiopian) amongst them. Only a handful are women, but many of those have young children. Some have been completely destroyed by their journey and cannot walk off the boat. A Red Cross volunteer must carry them down the stairs on his back. There are tears, including from a wailing toddler temporarily separated from her mother while she is accompanied off the boat. Most of the arrivals are completely shell-shocked and even fearful, barely responding to the instructions given by the volunteers.

When their feet touch the scorching concrete of the dock, some of them collapse into a heap and medics in gleaming white coats rush to their sides. Everyone is handed a pair of sandals and a small paper bag with a bottle of water and some snacks, before they are ushered to a large waiting tent. Volunteer doctors and nurses check their vitals, and then they are handed over to security officials, who collect identifying information. The whole thing takes ages and occurs in disturbing silence; for the most part the only sound we hear is the creaking boat and the cawing of the seagulls around us.

I remember clearly my first thought from these moments, because it cuts through the fog of my confusion so starkly: "They look like slaves." For some reason, when I looked at that boat and the people getting off it, I remembered all the images of human cargo that I had seen in museums in Zanzibar; in Elmira on Ghana's slave coast; all over Europe and North America. It's difficult to put the look into words—a vacant stare screaming that something essential has been taken from them, the shoulders slouched forward with an otherworldly resignation. The fact that they were on a cargo ship made the resonances sharper. Most of these people looked like they could be my age, maybe slightly younger. Many were unsteady on their feet. Confronted by the traumatised stares of my peers, stumbling through a strange place with nothing to their names but the clothes on their backs, I was struck by the thought that I was witnessing a funeral march of some kind, maybe for the friends who hadn't make it across—or maybe for the idea of Pan-Africanism itself.

Suddenly, the energy perked up as a hushed murmur rippled through the small crowd. The mayor was on his way. In my mind, I was expecting to encounter yet another hostile politician. With all the cameras pointed at him, I anticipated some slogan-eering. But I was pleasantly surprised. Leoluca Orlando wasn't there to posture or be intimidating. He was there because apparently he comes down to meet every boat that docks in Palermo, to reassure the people on board that the city will do whatever it can to help, before they are transferred to reception centres across the city. I wasn't really there to do the kind of in-depth research that needs to be done on this, or to write the kind of interview that needs to be written; but I saw the big difference that this small gesture made to the rescued people at the docks.

I managed to ask Orlando one or two questions in English, which he answered earnestly before speeding away.

This was Palermo. The story on the ground didn't neatly conform to the headline narratives I'd absorbed from the media. I expected far more xenophobia or racism than I got. More importantly, I saw ordinary people volunteer their time to receive people who had lost everything; to help them breathe a little easier, even if their breath was borrowed.

The same week as I was witnessing the arrival of the *Tuna I*, the Italian government announced that it was investigating charities and volunteer groups like the Nobel Prize-winning Médecins Sans Frontières for supporting these rescue missions on the high seas. According to Rome, by offering safe passage, these groups are collaborating with traffickers, and contravening official EU policy—in effect, to let migrants and refugees die as a form of "deterrence".

Why have European cities like Palermo become bastions of resistance to the painful harshness of EU migration policies? Why have Barcelona, Paris and others been opening up their doors to outsiders, while their national governments have raced over each other to be the harshest, the most closed-off, the most insulated? It might simply be because cities are smaller and experience the realities of human mobility more immediately than an abstract national government. A less benevolent interpretation might be that the black markets created by migrant trafficking offer pools of unregulated labour that keep the world's largest cities ticking over—those underpaid nail technicians and overworked supermarket assistants who inhale toxic fumes and do backbreaking work for endless hours on low pay must come from somewhere. It might be that cities foster empathy, because they are by definition diverse and multifaceted, and understand intimately the importance of multiculturalism for enriching daily life. Whatever the case, Palermo was one place where this was evident. There was an energy to the way the city rallied to receive the people who had been rescued that completely contradicted the screaming, angry rhetoric of the national administration.

* * *

I spent much of the rest of my time in Palermo talking to people who had survived the crossing and who were now in transitional housing in the city, praying for a chance at naturalisation or an opportunity to leave and head to other parts of Italy, or indeed Europe. While Italy as a whole is one of Europe's wealthier countries, the truth is that its economy has been floundering, particularly in the south, where there just isn't enough labour to sustain the intensive agriculture that makes the products for which Italy is best known. Olive groves and orange orchards are lying fallow as young people abandon the countryside for the big cities; those who manage to attend university face even more uncertainty, as they are too qualified to work the land, but not qualified enough to secure the increasingly rare white-collar office work they crave. In fact, most of the volunteers that I met at the sea that day were precisely that: university graduates for whom the Mediterranean crisis had opened up an unexpected opportunity for work.

From Kenya, I tried three times to volunteer directly with reception centres for African arrivals in Greece and Italy, and twice was unable to make the project happen because I didn't have the patience to navigate the vagaries of the Schengen system. Volunteering in this way would have been considered working, which is prohibited by the Schengen tourist visa. This is partly why the crisis of the Mediterranean has descended into a conversation between Europeans. It is European governments putting in place the inhumane policies on the water, just as it is European humanitarian organisations—staffed almost entirely by European volunteers—that intervene on the rescue ships and on the docks. It is as if Europe has decided the terms of the debate that it must have within itself, blocking out any sort of perspective from the other side of the sea.

At the docks in Palermo, the contradictions of European humanitarianism were apparent. Aside from the small cluster of volunteers, there was a large assembly of European security services—the local police, the coast guard, detectives. The volunteers I spoke to in Palermo saw themselves as responding to a humanitarian imperative that was difficult to separate from their European identity. "I came because I had been volunteering with refugees at my university, and even though I had never been to Palermo before, I was curious about what happens at the dock," one young law student told me, using the extended wait between finishing her law degree and studying for the bar to volunteer as an intercultural mediator with the Italian Red Cross.

Local leaders like Mayor Orlando see the crisis in the Mediterranean as the gravest humanitarian crisis Europe has ever faced. "I am convinced that, in fifty years, European governments will be facing prosecution for crimes against humanity," he told me while overseeing the reception of the *Tuna I*. Like his counterpart in Barcelona, Orlando has taken on the cause of migrants and refugees arriving in his city as a moral rather than a political question—a question about the kind of future that Europe wants to have a hand in creating.

* * *

A few weeks after I left Palermo, I tendered my resignation and took some time away from humanitarian work to do more independent research. I was facing a future of uncertainty—of trying to define my place in a world that had shown me that people who looked like me could be allowed to die just to score political points. It is difficult to explain the difference between reading about a crisis and witnessing it. It is equally difficult to explain what it feels like when you look directly into the eyes of someone whose life could have been yours, had only two or three of your circumstances been different. When I looked into the eyes of all those people carried off that boat or collapsing on the ground, I hadn't seen an object of pity. I'd seen myself with some details adjusted, and I just couldn't go back to pretending that being a bureaucrat would be enough. I am different because I saw how tenuous any privilege that might be accorded to me really was, in a world where the most powerful governments in the world would rather let people who look like me die as a point of principle.

Significantly, I left Italy thinking about empathy as a political value. As a human rights practitioner with a legal background, I had always wrestled with the way that practising in this field seemed to invite abstraction: that even the people who were supposedly on the frontline of defending the world's most vulnerable were supposed to pretend that their work was driven purely by abstract facts, and not by the human connections that exist between people, whether they know it or not. Especially as a black woman working in this space, I've often felt tremendous pressure to "leave myself out" of the work in a way that I am no longer sure is healthy, or right. The subtle messaging within the human rights space is that the white man is the natural occupant of this domain; for anyone else to participate, you must either accept your role as a perpetual inferior, or progressively switch off all of the impulses that you've collected from experiencing the world in a different way. You must pretend that you have never encountered racism. You must act as if sexism is not an issue. You must pretend that European colonisation never happened. And what you are left with is a runt of yourself, contorted to fit other people's expectations and unable to fulfil the calling that put you on that path in the first place.

In practice, my Palermo epiphany set a countdown clock on my work for other organisations too. I couldn't un-see it, and I couldn't find any organisation that was both willing to let me do the work I had been called to do and to make space for all the aspects of my identity that had driven me towards the work. I kept thinking about the difference between a white man pitching up in my home country of Kenya on a tourist visa to "volunteer", with all the power and access that he would be afforded there, and myself, standing on that dock in Palermo, secretly and shamefully hoping that the police wouldn't confuse me for one of the people who had disembarked. I kept thinking about the dynamics of privilege and identity that quietly define the scope people are given to be useful in this work. And I realised that I had to pick my battles. I had to decide if I was going to spend the best years of my life fighting to change organisations that might ultimately decide not to change; or whether, like Edward Said, I would embrace the current of being the intellectual in exile—perpetually excluded, untethered but not unmoored, floating towards a bigger intellectual goal, even at the expense of short-term professional achievement.

And so I left.

6

LOOKING FOR BESSIE

The first time I encounter Bessie Head, I am a teenager struggling to memorise the reams and binders of information that Kenyan high school students are expected to learn and regurgitate for their national exams. She is nestled in an edited collection that we read for English Literature, and even though her story "Looking for a Rain God" gives the collection its name, we skip through it briskly. Our English teacher is struggling. Head's themes are not easy and her story is unsettling. Like most of the other African narratives we encounter, it is set in a village—this time in rural Botswana—and a little family is facing the worst ever drought in a country with a long history of drought. But, unlike any of the other stories that we will ever read, Head's characters do not respond to their challenges in a way that allows readers to derive a simple, pat moral arc. If she has anything to teach us from this short story, it is that human beings are complex and, in their complexity and desire to survive, they can do the vilest things. It is clear that the English teacher isn't sure if she should be teaching such a violent and disturbing story to a gaggle of teenage girls at a Catholic high school.

TRAVELLING WHILE BLACK

The second time I encounter Bessie Head, I am at university, taking a class on African literature as part of my graduate degree in African Studies. It is an eight-week course taught across the English and African Studies departments, but after six weeks the English students drift back towards Chaucer and Shakespeare, while we, the three African Studies students, plough on with our Achebe and Soyinka. The reading list is hefty. We read three or four full-length novels or non-fiction books a week, for two one-hour discussions; because the class is small, each of us can expect at least one question every week. So we absolutely have to do the reading.

On the first day after the English students have taken the bend in the river back to Shakespeare, we meet as usual. At the end of class, one of the others asks our male lecturer a simple question that changes everything: why haven't we read any books written by women?

It is true. We have powered through twenty-four books that are supposed to represent the best writing from and about the continent—Achebe, Soyinka, Ngũgĩ and even Naipaul—but we have not read a single book written by a woman. So the instructor, duly ashamed, returns with the last six books for the class, all by or about women. Nadine Gordimer. Doris Lessing. Mariama Bâ. And nestled in this penance list is Bessie Head and her most complex work of all, her semi-autobiographical novel *A Question of Power*.

We read Gordimer, Lessing and Head together, as examples of women's writing in apartheid South Africa. I don't warm to Gordimer's *Burger's Daughter*. I read it and feel the significance of the story, but I don't connect to it in the way I would have expected. I think now this was in part because it wasn't the right time. I think it was also because I found the characters a little too abstract for a political situation that I found to be quite urgent and real. I was in the middle of my political awakening, and I just wasn't ready to receive Gordimer. Lessing I found opaque and difficult to finish. In fact, as I write this, I still have never finished reading *The Golden Notebook*. When I tell people this, they often react with horror and remind me that it is one of the greatest feminist novels of our time. That's probably true. But that doesn't mean I have to like it as a book. I just didn't have the visceral reaction to it that I was expected to. Books are like that. If the right book enters your life at the wrong moment, it can leave you cold and underwhelmed. But at the right moment, it can change everything.

For me, Bessie Head's *A Question of Power* was the right book entering my life at exactly the right time—when I was ready to receive it. I was at Oxford, experiencing the dislocation and disjuncture of entering a place with a long history of publicly and viscerally rejecting people like me. The first black students were admitted to Oxford in the early twentieth century, but they were all men, and they were scattered, few and far between. Many developed severe mental health issues as the rigid institution, with its eccentric habits and expectations, gnawed away at their sense of self and purpose. The dates for the admission of women are tricky, because some colleges always allowed women to attend or be affiliated, but the last all-male college to admit women did so in 1985. The relics of the university's history of exclusion surround you and are often subtly interwoven in the ways people speak to and about you. Walking around the halls of Oxford as a black African woman was a constant lesson in alienation; of being constantly and fundamentally outside your peace.

Alienation and disorientation are two of the things Bessie Head writes about in *A Question of Power*. The novel is about herself in South Africa in the 1960s, but she may as well have been hiding in the corridors and tutorial rooms of Oxford, taking notes while African students survive and negotiate the politics of the place. She changed everything for me. She didn't fix anything, but suddenly I had camaraderie in my isolation and otherness. More importantly, after years and years of having African literature with an overt and unsubtle morality shoved down my throat through intellectual laziness and lack of creativity, here was Bessie Head. She's not trying to teach us anything or fix the world. She just wants us to sit with her for a while, as she tells us what it feels like to lose a handle on reality and on one's sense of self. I was hooked.

And so the third time I encountered Bessie Head, as a working adult, was a homecoming. I was returning to a long-loved one, and having African literature given back to me. If the canon used Achebe and Ngũgĩ to suggest that all Africans are the same, then for the rest of us who could never quite lie low enough or blend in completely, we had Bessie Head. It was the difference between a grand metanarrative of African identity and the smallness of single stories that help individuals find their place in the enormity of history.

During this time, I was going through a period of intense professional upheaval. I decided to do an experiment. Following the lead of a columnist at the website Writers of Colour, I decided not to read books written by white men for a year. The point was to force ourselves to read outside the canon, to read outside the narrow categories that power prescribes for us. The point was to expand the reader's horizons. Like most literature-lovers, I had been uncritically consuming "great works" of literature without understanding that the metrics for greatness reflect the biases of the people who create them. Yes, there are measures of quality that we might be able to agree upon across difference, but greatness? Greatness is loaded with subjectivity and the preferences of power. I wanted to challenge myself and these presumptions of what it means to be great in one swoop, so I joined the commitment.

Bessie Head's *Maru* was one of the first novels I read during this experiment. I found it in an unexpected bookshop in

Nairobi—a brand new copy for $3.50. In Kenya books are taxed as luxury goods, and that can mean taxes of up to 60 per cent of the book's value, not to mention the costs of the retailer and the importer tagged on. It is possible for a book in Kenya, imported from India, the UK or the US, to cost up to three times its list price. So when I found all these Bessie Head books on sale at $2.50 or $3.50 a piece, I was blown away and I bought them all. *Maru. The Cardinals. When Rain Clouds Gather.* I couldn't wait to get into them, and she absolutely did not disappoint. By the end of the one and a half years of the experiment, I had read almost seventy books. Some were forgettable. Some were disturbing. But then there was Bessie Head, who changed everything.

I read *Maru* in two hours. *When Rain Clouds Gather* took another two and a half. I was in tears. I was moved in such an elemental way. I can't explain it—I think I actually physically felt my soul shift within my spirit. There was a restlessness in my heart that had not been there before. But not a negative restlessness. I would describe it as the yearning you get when you've had the best meal or the best glass of wine in your life, and you spend the rest of your days in every restaurant you visit, trying to find that taste again. Your concept of what it means to taste or feel has shifted and can never go back. Suddenly the horizon of possibility when it comes to taste have been opened, and the prospect of going back to reading something that doesn't move you like this terrifies you. That is what it felt like to read *Maru* for that first time.

I'm not sure when the idea started taking shape that I now had to go and retrace Bessie Head's life. I think it has something to do with what her literature did for me. Edward Said says that it is the people with a spiritual or intellectual disposition, leaving them constantly feeling like outsiders, who are best placed to look at their societies—they can do it from a place of abstraction that makes their analysis sharper or clearer. "Exiles cross borders," he wrote, "break barriers of thought and experience". Both Said and Head were on the outside looking in, and because of their outsider status were able to see the world with a sharp intellectual and moral clarity. Bessie Head was an exile, and I too had grown up with a deep sense of spiritual exile or fundamental outsider-ness that drove me towards both travel and writing. I think in some way my spirit knew that the journey to find the arc of Bessie Head's life would be as close to a homecoming as I would ever get.

* * *

Alice Walker once went in search of Zora Neale Hurston, and wrote an essay about it. The premise of the essay is easy: it follows Walker to Eatonville, Hurston's hometown, which remembers its favourite daughter with a qualified warmth. She is one of them, but in a distant, and abstract way. They don't know the famous Zora, only their daughter, aunt and friend. Zora, from around the way. But for Walker, and eventually for millions of readers around the world, Hurston would become a beacon for what the written word was and could be. She was an unqualified genius.

Zora Neale Hurston was an African American anthropologist and novelist who was in her prime during the Harlem Renaissance, but was somehow found to be too weird, too vocal and altogether too strong for the men who saw themselves as the standard-bearers for the times. It was one of those things where men appoint themselves as the gatekeepers of a subculture, and women must either conform to those gatekeeping standards or be confined to the dregs of history. Hurston wasn't the only female writer of the period who suffered that fate. Dorothy West, author of *The Living is Easy* and *The Wedding*, wrote at around the same time, but her second novel was not published until 1995, because her themes were considered too patrician and not radical enough for the civil rights era.

Hurston's prose sparkles with her keen eye for observation, sharpened no doubt by her experiences as an anthropologist, as well as a strong sense of kinship and solidarity with her characters. Her masterpiece, *Their Eyes Were Watching God*, is a masterclass in writing in dialect—letting characters speak the way they would, and not necessarily in a way that your audience would understand; trusting that eventually your audience will catch on and stay with you. She didn't write very much, and some of her books were lost for almost the entire second half of the twentieth century, because we readers were consumed by her male contemporaries like Langston Hughes and James Baldwin. *Barracoon*, Hurston's biography of the last person brought over to the United States as a slave, was only published in 2018.

Alice Walker's 1975 essay "Looking for Zora" gave Hurston back to the world. Walker documents her experience of going out to the Florida swamps to seek out the last remaining people who remember Hurston—her long-lost relatives who, it seems, did not understand how significant she was to the American literary canon. The essay triggered a wave of rediscovery, and suddenly Hurston was everywhere. Alice Walker gave one of the strongest, clearest voices of its era back to us.

I had this essay at the back of my mind in December 2017, when I finally made my way to Botswana. I genuinely don't even remember why or how I came to read it. It's not an easy piece to find; you can only get scanned copies online. But I had, and it had such deep resonances for me. At the time, I had just returned to Kenya after eleven years abroad, and the honeymoon period was long over. Everything in the country was becoming just that little bit more difficult and complicated. In my middle-class neighbourhood, there was only water in the taps one day a week, if at all. Once a week, without fail, the electricity would go out—from 9 a.m. to 5 p.m. On those days, I could not work from home. And every Sunday, through the distorted buzzing of

93

criminally old loudspeakers, a chorus of competing churches bellowed their praises to a God seemingly hard of hearing.

Kenya was pushing me to think critically about what it meant to be home. We love to tell ourselves these beautiful stories about how we all have homelands because we all come from somewhere; but, the older I get, the more I question these fairy tales. Some of us are away from home because it mangles up our sense of self and continuously spits us out. Some people find home in journeys and travel, in disconnection and transience. For some people, home is not a geography but a state of mind—it's wherever they can do work that feels meaningful or useful. Reading that essay, and speaking with Alice Walker, who I consider to be one of the greatest literary voices ever, I saw in her something that most writers recognise. Where home isn't a place, but is in the ever-changing community or fellowship of people who see the world the way you do, and find the words to describe it. Finding Zora Neale Hurston helped Alice Walker find herself, and while I can't remember the precise moment of inspiration, this began to make me think that I could find myself too.

I ended up thinking about the trip for at least three years. It finally took shape when the 2017 election took enough of a toll on my mind and my spirit that I knew I had to do something purely out love and interest. I can't give you a good reason for why it was suddenly important for me to find Bessie Head, except that the election left me completely depleted and disoriented. After eleven years on the road, my ideas of home had become incredibly fluid, but I think on some level I had always held on to an idea of permanence in Kenya. Yet everything that happened during the election reminded me that home was more than just a place. When an election costs you friends and even family because you are the wrong ethnic group, you start to question more than just the outcome of the vote. Here was Bessie Head, a female writer who had been vomited by her own country because of her sense of justice. And there I was, a female writer violently reminded that my peace in my home country was wildly contingent. I needed to make a pilgrimage.

I had been to Botswana before, but I had never been to Serowe, where Bessie Head lived and wrote. And I had been to South Africa before, but never to her birthplace of Maritzburg. I was a broken writer following the footsteps of another broken writer; but where she had been pushed on her journey by circumstance and history, I was choosing mine. Bessie was my complete break from Kenyan politics. She gave me something to work towards that wasn't the gore and guts of men fighting for power. I could barely afford this trip, but when I described it to a friend who was working as an editor, he was the first person who saw what it could be, and figured out a way to get me a small advance. I had to figure out the rest myself.

I couldn't just buy a plane ticket and go, given South Africa's strict policies: without an official invitation there was no way the government would have given me a visa. But when you have a so-called weak passport, you become expert at creating and using visa windows to see more of the world—a small act to reclaim whatever freedoms are left over after the stronger passports have had their fill. Once again, I extended a work trip to South Africa to allow myself some time to make this journey. A few clicks, and we're off.

* * *

Head was born in Pietermaritzburg, KwaZulu-Natal, and spent the first three decades of her life in South Africa. I had already been to Johannesburg, Cape Town and Durban—the three South African economic hubs—but I was curious to see if the town known to locals as Maritzburg or PMB would be different. Maritzburg is unknown to many outside South Africa, because it is eclipsed by larger, nearby Durban. The fissures of apartheid still ripple through the town, and evidence that Bessie was here has fallen into the resulting cracks. Maritzburg was initially a black town and then came the Indian community, which was summarily displaced to make room for a white settler community. The centre today is an eclectic mix of modern buildings and Dutch-inspired architecture, littered with statues of Queen Victoria, as well as a bustling market. Like many other South African towns, the white population has abandoned the town centre and taken many of the public services with it, and so the genteel facade that allowed the racist administration to make peace with its own ugliness has worn away.

This was Bessie Head's birthplace, at a time when the regime was concocting its racist violence. She was mixed-race, with a white mother and a black father she never knew, born into a white family that did not want her. I planned to spend two full days in Maritzburg, visiting the sanatorium where she was born, or the school where she studied, or the one where she taught—anything that would give me a sense of the things that made her who she became. I wasn't sure what to expect. Pietermaritzburg's name itself, in the heart of Zulu country, screams colonisation and domination. One of the first acts of independence in a lot of African countries was to rename towns and cities—unfortunately, mostly after the big man of the day. In Kenya, Kingsway became Kenyatta Avenue. The Prince of Wales School became the Nairobi School. Is Maritzburg still Maritzburg because of political inertia, or is there something more significant about South Africa's incomplete decolonisation? The town itself shows a complex legacy, with its neoclassical buildings and statues of Queen Victoria, including a dominating redbrick city council building, surrounded by a minibus (taxi) station, and the inevitable small market growing around them.

Bessie Head grew into adulthood in this town and the fact that almost all traces of her life here have been erased is a testament to the structural violence of apartheid. At the time of her birth, Maritzburg was a cornerstone of the project: an African homeland forcibly separated from its heritage and countryside and sharply divided along racial lines. Maritzburg was the site of numerous forced displacements of both the African and Indian populations to make room for new white settlements. Many buildings that would have been at the centre of people's lives until the 1970s are simply gone, and as a result it's hard to find traces of Bessie. Family records suggest that her mother was placed in an asylum because of her mixed-race union with Bessie's black father. Under the apartheid laws, interracial sex was criminalised, and risked arrest or even death for the black half of the couple.

By the time she left Maritzburg for Johannesburg and then Cape Town, Head was already writing. She joined a small magazine and filed both fiction and non-fiction stories which paid little. She met a young man and married him, and they had a son together, but she never really loved him and their marriage fell apart quickly. Writing remained her only true love, even when it failed to provide her with any kind of comfort. She tried teaching, but despite the promise of financial security, she was unable to give up her calling to the page. While in Cape Town, she flirted with anti-apartheid organising, but a violent police raid and subsequent surveillance left her shaken. She also survived a sexual assault during this time that seemed to sour her completely on the liberation movement. If Head was going to taste freedom, she felt like she was going to do so on her own.

The apartheid government tried very hard to erase Bessie Head and other black writers, and by the end of my three-day stay in Maritzburg, I simply haven't had enough time to do the kind of digging required to find people who might have known her as a child, or documents that trace the contours of her life. I visit the small town's museum and take in a stirring installation on the impact of racial segregation on the people of Maritzburg. I try to access official records at the council registry, but they tell me that I would need far more time than I have. So I wander around the town centre, absorbing the contradictions of Maritzburg, wondering if I should give up now and go back to Johannesburg. And then on the second to last day, as I am walking through the main street I turn a corner—just past the taxi station and the small market—and I see it, in giant black cursive letters against a bold pink background.

The Bessie Head Public Library.

In July 2007, thirty-one years after she died, the main library at Pietermaritzburg was renamed after Bessie Head. I'm not sure I have ever been in another library in Africa named for a woman, let alone a major library in a major town. The library itself is small, and its tribute to Bessie is simple: a collection of all the books she published and all the books published about her, in a glass case at the centre of the first floor. To me, it is magnificent, and I am slightly overcome with emotion. I talk to a librarian who knows Head's work well, and they allow me to sit and be in her presence all afternoon long. All week I have been trying to find evidence that Bessie was here—the sanatorium where she was abandoned is gone, as is the hospital, the orphanage where she grew up has long since been converted into something else. But here is proof that she is of Maritzburg. She left the town in such frustration, but came back in a form that she probably would have loved: as a temple to the books that she loved and that saved her. I feel, for the first time since I began this strange journey, that I am on the right track.

* * *

In 1964, Head left South Africa for Botswana on an exit permit, in circumstances consistent with the state's determination to beat her down. As part of the restrictions on black people's freedom of movement, the apartheid regime allowed non-white South Africans seen to be politically active to leave and never return. Essentially, unless the country they went to nationalised them, these people were rendered stateless. This is exactly what happened to Bessie Head, who had her citizenship violently torn away at 27 years old and spent most of the second half of her life looking for a sense of home in Botswana.

I followed her footsteps from Maritzburg north to Botswana's capital, Gaborone. Botswana is an interesting place. The whole country has a quiet, placid energy that those of us who come from big cities struggle with. The first time I visited, I was supposed to be there for three days—I left after one and a half. Having just come over from the big-city energy of Johannesburg and Nairobi, Gaborone had felt like a small town that I just couldn't get a handle on. Ten years later as I tracked down Bessie Head, the city was growing considerably, although still a significant change for anyone arriving from one of the neighbouring large towns. Most of the country is the Kalahari desert, and the small population—at the time of writing there were twice as many people in Nairobi as in all of Botswana—makes even the capital feel like a small town.

I take a small local bus to Serowe, hunched in the front seat behind the driver with my rucksack underneath my feet. I read somewhere once that this is the safest seat on any bus, because when the driver panics their first instinct is going to be to save themselves. Serowe was where Bessie did most of her writing. In her books, Serowe is a small rural village with a single school and a habit of gossip. In 2017, Serowe is a large town. I had no idea where I was going, except that a website that hadn't been updated in years assured me there was a Khama II Museum in Serowe where Bessie Head's personal papers are housed. Thankfully, I had over a decade of backpacking experience behind me and so the disorientation was not overwhelming. I don't know why I picked the hotel that I did, in a location that forced me to walk the same road back and forth multiple times a day between the room and the town. I wish I could explain it, but only later would I realise that stories like this are often bigger than we realise.

When I first pitched my editor a story about Bessie Head, it was in part because I am trying to make sense of my own awkward introduction to her genius. Stumbling into Bessie Head's magic the way I did ignited an insatiable curiosity in me. Her work stands apart. I have read everything she has published and it was still not enough—she died young and perhaps at the peak of her acclaim, leaving us hungry for more. I must find more Bessie Head to satisfy the sense of kinship I find in her writing: our shared desire to protect our writing from being subsumed by the restrictive ideas of what makes a sequence of words "African". So when I learn of her letters at the museum, it is as if a portal has opened to a secret playground that I always sensed existed even without proof. A door has opened to the mind and heart of this woman whose words have left an indelible mark on my own work as a writer and on my consciousness as a reader. I must find Bessie Head.

The Khama II Museum is a small nondescript building at the edge of Serowe, about ten minutes off the main road and a full six and a half hours away from Gaborone. Behind the dense tree line surrounding the small complex is a small but smooth-running operation hosting two remarkable collections. The museum contains the personal and family papers of the Khama dynasty—the leading family of the Bangamwato people that has ruled Botswana intermittently since before independence, and has given modern Botswana two presidents. The first of these, Sir Seretse Khama, not only negotiated Botswana's independence from South Africa but also helped the country navigate the complexities of being a frontline state during the war against apartheid. But in the same pristine three-roomed archive are stacks of plain, grey-green boxes, arranged neatly in alphanumeric order, that contain the private letters of Botswana's best-known author.

The letters are far more than anything I could have hoped for. Bessie Head is, and perhaps more so in private than in her published writing, a conflagration of passion and talent, battling state-sponsored psychological terror and the corporate writing establishment from her two-roomed house in Serowe. "Merciful God," she writes to her agent, "make me more alert about death from the teeth of big business. May they not send their agents here to kill me. In me still grows the great novel that changes the world, but tenderly, tenderly." Here was a writer who fully occupied her genius and wielded it as a weapon against the omnipresent, crushing weight of the political moment in which she lived and wrote.

People who study Africa have always been deeply fascinated by Botswana, and the idea of this exceptional place that defies typical perceptions of Africa. If Africa is dysfunctional, then Botswana is functional. If Africa is dark and scary, then Botswana is inviting and bathed in light. If the rest of Africa is poor, then Botswana is not. But when you talk to people who are actually from Botswana, the picture is always a little more complicated than it seems. The country has a tremendous and well-earned reputation for being democratic and open, but inequalities and a frail thread of repression run through some of the national policies.

Bessie Head was at the receiving end of this. As a frontline state in the war against apartheid—sharing a border with South Africa—Botswana received both dissidents and exiles, as well as attacks organised by the South African National Defence Force. From the 1960s to the 1980s, there were bombings and attempted assassinations across the Kalahari, from Namibia to Mozambique, allegedly including the assassination of Mozambican president Samora Machel. If the regime felt that a neighbouring country was hostile, or supporting the ANC, retaliation would swiftly follow.

Apartheid Johannesburg feverishly embraced free-market capitalism to gain a measure of patronage and protection from the United States during the worst of the Cold War years, and because Botswana was also capitalist in a region that had swung towards communism, there was somewhat more South African co-operation with Gaborone than with Mozambique or Angola. As a result, Botswana let in South African exiles on the premise that they would quickly move on to other countries, so as not to antagonise the apartheid regime. Refugee and asylum policy was designed to discourage resettlement within the territory. This is why Bessie Head, fleeing the storms of racism, did not receive citizenship for fifteen years. Today, Botswana celebrates her as its greatest writer, but every Monday for fifteen years she had to report to the local police station to show that she was not in breach of her refugee status. She had to plead with the government for travel documents every time she wanted to go abroad to speak or to study. You see in her letters that statelessness was disorienting and humiliating, even if it inspired the stark beauty of her work.

And statelessness was just one of the many indignities that Head struggled with in Botswana. Loneliness and debilitating poverty loomed large over her work and her private correspondence. Head was an insatiable letter-writer—and why wouldn't she be? Stuck in a village, without the entertainments that many writers use to inoculate themselves against the isolated writing life, sending letters was probably the only way for her to connect with people who understood her life's work. As much as we idealise the writer as a solitary figure, good writing does require a measure of connection. A good writer needs people on whom they can test out their ideas, or from whom they can draw inspiration. You might feel alone and alienated, but it is in that reach for community that most writers realise their calling.

For the first few years in Serowe, Head was an outsider. Most of the people in the small village thought she was white because she was mixed-race, and assumed that she had money, which she didn't. In fact, she was incredibly poor, and got poorer still as the vagaries of the writing world collided with the idiosyncrasies of life in a small town in a small country. Money was always a problem, and Head frequently had to beg the local bank for advances or loans while she was waiting for her publisher to send her money from the UK. She relied on soirees or meet-ups in Gaborone for physical connection with other writers and only had two people in Serowe that she counted as friends. Really, writing her books and letters was her only true connection to the literary world.

The letters reveal inequalities within the writing world that still persist today. Bessie was black, she was a woman, and she was African, and each of these identities combined into a specific, intersectional marginalisation that may eventually have killed her. At the time she wrote, the white publishing world was congratulating itself on the discovery of Achebe, Soyinka and other male African writers, but even those few had to battle for the respect and attention they deserved. Publishers like Toni Morrison (at the time an editor at Random House) tried to champion the African writer; but, much like today, there was a sense that there could only be one. So even though writers like Head were producing glorious works of fiction and non-fiction, their works were treated as marginal or superfluous, particularly in the United States.

As a woman, Head experienced this particularly keenly. I think back to that African Literature class and I see what the outside world sees when they look at African writing. A litany of male philosopher-kings pontificating about the contest between African patriarchy and European patriarchy, unfeeling or unseeing of the voices of women, queer people and those who don't fit the mould.

The publication of African literature has been violently gendered. Even though African women have always written, the voice of men is often portrayed as neutral, while women's voices are considered "special interest". The stories of everyday suffering written by men are considered universal, but the unique experiences of women and queer people are treated as peculiar or particular.

This remains true today. When I was pitching my first non-fiction book to publishers around the world, including in Africa, people struggled with the idea of an African woman as a non-fiction writer. How would we market you? How would we position you? Is there any chance that you write fiction? Women writing is strange enough, but women writing through the experience women is still treated as special-interest.

This was the world in which Head sought to establish herself. She tried to connect, first with the men of the US African American literary set in the 1950s—but they had little time for an African woman writer. She reached out to African male writers like Achebe and Ngũgĩ as well, but their responses were curt and perfunctory. White writers like Nadine Gordimer and Doris Lessing sent money, but very little of themselves. Only when she was in Serowe, writing to women like Alice Walker, Nikki Giovanni and Toni Morrison, was Bessie able to start etching out a place for herself amongst the literary set. She was still marginal relative to their prosperity and their acceptance among urbane audiences, but at least she was in the room.

It's no wonder that literature professors don't know what to do with Bessie Head. Here was a writer who actually lived in remote rural Africa, instead of just imagining it from behind a typewriter in a city. When Head looked out into the African village as a setting for her stories, she didn't just see cartoonish, one-dimensional characters fulfilling whatever predetermined trope the writer needed them to feel. She saw people, in all their complexities and their difficulty. Head didn't see the village as a static imaginary background to a morality tale that urban Africans losing their way needed to read before they lost their way completely. She saw real people whose existence was not dependent on whether the urban spaces saw them or did not.

I think that, because much of the writing world does not know how to see Africa, and much of urban Africa struggles with the complexities of rurality, writers like Bessie Head have had and continue to fight to find their place. I think we all have stories we tell ourselves about who we are and our place in the world, and when we encounter people who challenge that, we find it easier to ignore them altogether than to change our stereotypes and perceptions in order to accommodate them. I think this is what happened to Bessie Head. "An isolated goddamn outsider trying to be an African of Africa," she once called herself, or, as I've described her elsewhere, a city girl stuck in a village, a South African forced to build a life in Botswana, a woman outside traditional norms of womanhood, an intellectual living in a village with limited basic education facilities, and a human being who struggled with mental ill health almost all her life.

Eventually, being trebly marginalised in this way took its toll on Bessie Head. The letters I read in Serowe show that ritualised humiliation at the hands of the state took a toll on her mental health. She was angry and frustrated, but Botswana would not listen until it was far too late. She couldn't make ends meet— even enough to put piped water in her home—and fetching water back and forth destroyed her back. She had a terrible relationship with the father of her only child, although she eventually sent the young man, Howard, to live with his father. And, just when the tide was turning, when someone finally saw in her books a voice worth preserving and elevating, Bessie Head died, poor, sick and alone.

* * *

In August 1973, when Alice Walker went to Eatonville, Florida in search of Zora Neale Hurston, she was looking for a novelist who burnt brilliantly for a season only to die in poverty and relative obscurity. Writing is such a powerful medium that can do so much for the world, and I think most of us have this belief that writers should be—must, surely, be—handsomely rewarded for their time and their craft. We see the headline news of a select few writers getting six-figure book deals and high-profile celebrity endorsements, and we think that's how it's supposed to be. In a world where public intellectuals give order to our political consciousness, we imagine that the intellectual able to commit their thoughts to paper, and to almost fully incorporate themselves into our psyche, must be wealthy or at least comfortable.

In Hurston, Walker found what all writers know to be true, and certainly what I am now finding to be true for Head: fame in writing almost never translates into material wealth, and your favourite writer is often one tragedy or one mishap away from dying penniless and getting lost in the annals of time. Of the tens of thousands of books published around the world every year, only a handful enter the canon; and of those handful only ten or twenty will make the author enough of a return to allow them to continue writing. Especially writers who are following that nagging demon voice that tells them they must write. Those people are not writing books that will sell in airport bookshops or be recommended by celebrity book clubs. Those writers are lucky if they can pay rent.

This was the tragedy of Hurston and Head. Hurston's *Their Eyes Were Watching God*, written in masterful dialect, is a magical tribute to African Americans escaping violent racism in the South only to battle colourism and racism's subsidiary infections. Head wrote love letters to rural Africa that could not be collapsed handily into the tropes that both urban Africa and the Western world had cultivated, with an insatiable appetite for suffering that Africans craved. Langston Hughes called Hurston "the most amusing [among New York's] 'Niggerati'", a tepid recognition of Hurston's singularity. When Bessie Head asked for his help in getting a book about apartheid South Africa published, he asked his agent to blow her off.

In fact, like Hurston, Head had the disorienting experience of not having a canon in Botswana that she could reach into for belonging, having been vomited by apartheid South Africa and not being considered the right kind of African for the male-dominated publishing space of the 1960s and '70s. She found that the African American Harlem clique had little time for an African village woman. This strange misunderstanding still persists today. African writers seek kinship from African American writers and, instead of finding solidarity and a sense of belonging, they are made to feel doubly marginalised. The black diaspora refracted through the lens of racism and imperialism makes it difficult for black writers to see each other properly and on their own terms; and so we see partial versions of each other that make it impossible to collaborate. Many writers like Hughes and Giovanni were dismissive of Head and her Africa-centred stories—only Toni Morrison and Alice Walker seemed to see the genius in her.

Walker talks of being drawn to Zora's spirit and being compelled to bring her back from obscurity, saving us from losing her. She writes about stumbling around the overgrown Eatonville cemetery, calling out to Hurston—pleading with her to show herself. I understand this compulsion, because it is what pushes me to rip through my savings in search of the consciousness of Bessie Head. I have no guarantees that an essay on my quest will be published. I have no reason to head to Serowe, other than I must. And on the last day of my trip I also find myself stumbling through an overgrown cemetery, looking for an obscure and overgrown grave-marker choking under a knot of weeds.

Walker was also one of Bessie's correspondents, and the letters she pens to her are soaked in her love for other black women writers. A year after she went in search of Hurston, Walker was exchanging letters with Bessie Head: warm, effusive, vast missives in praise of each other's writing and personhood. In fact, Walker provided a back cover quote for the US edition of *A Question of Power*. Theirs was a sisterhood of letters, knitting together a kinship beyond national or social boundaries. Of a collection of short stories that Walker shared for feedback, Head wrote, "I don't know when these notes are ever going to get done as every now and then I have to stop writing and go and lie down on the floor prostrate with worship."

I reach out to Walker, because I want to better understand this kinship. And I admit I am pleasantly surprised that she responds with such candour and depth. "I became interested in African writers partly because an older sister had travelled to and taught in Nigeria when I was small," she tells me, adding, "as a student at Spelman my best friend, Constance Nabwire, was from Uganda. There was also a lot of interest at that time, the Sixties, in the 'real' Africa as opposed to the racist myths most Americans grew up on." When Walker finally left Mississippi and found work as an editor at *Ms.* magazine, she was at last in a position to support the writers whose work she loved: "I knew I must make an effort to find these writers and to publish them in the US. I felt a great sisterhood with all of the African women writers I was able to edit and publish."

But Head and Walker's correspondence goes beyond mere fascination. From great distance, they support each other through tremendously difficult personal moments. Walker shares that she knew from the moment she picked up Head's stories that this was a singular talent. "Bessie was special because she is special," she tells me, "each story she sent moved me. And when I learned of her history, in South Africa, the fate of her parents, the way she was treated in Botswana, I realized I was connected to a very special being and that it was my duty to stand, in whatever ways I could, with her." And stand with her she did—meeting with Head in New York while the latter was wrapping up her stay at the Iowa Writer's Workshop in 1976. When things were getting particularly dire for Head financially, Walker tried to help her find a writing fellowship somewhere in the US that would at least give her room to breathe. They scrambled and almost got there, but unfortunately Head died before she could take up Walker's offer.

"She just seemed to go very deep into the souls and subconscious of her characters," Walker enthuses. "Her work has a gravity, a depth, that startles and in some cases transforms the reader. In that sense it is as if she gave voice to a part of Creation itself—rural Africa and a largely unknown group of people—that was lacking enough attention, or literary oxygen, to stay alive."

Yet, for all her genius and her relative fame, Bessie Head died poor. The constant theme in her life's arc was defiance—of expectations, of boundaries, and of intellectual limitations. Head left a secure job in teaching to make a go of writing based on nothing but a blind belief in her talent. She refused to let the indignities of apartheid box her in, and when it became too much, she left. When publishers tried to undersell her work, she told them plainly to fuck off. But that defiance ultimately cost her the fame and relative fortune that was showered on her African contemporaries. Although her books tore through the global literary scene, demanding the attention of readers and industry gatekeepers, after an agent with his own literary ambitions mismanaged her affairs she was forced to beg contemporaries like Lessing and Gordimer, really anyone who would listen, for money. The profits from her first novel *When Rain Clouds Gather* allowed her to build herself a house named after it, but the name may as well have been a prophecy. The roof of Rain

Clouds leaked incessantly and, as she poured a small fortune into fixing it, Bessie broke her back fetching buckets of water for herself and her son Howard. The back injury of course triggered more financial issues, as did a permanently broken-down fridge.

Ultimately, Bessie Head's is a story about the futility of genius in the absence of privilege. Writers can be very dishonest about the privileges that make their lives possible. I was only able to write my first book and make a real go of this profession because I moved back home; for almost a year and a half my only real bills were the Internet and electricity. But even that is nothing compared to the opportunities afforded to people already famous for something else. They, already armed with a team of highly paid agents and publicists, will have access that the ordinary author thinks is organic, but is actually part of a well-oiled machine. Writing as a career is about networks and privilege, and the rare story of the person who makes it despite it all is rare for a reason—because it just doesn't happen that often.

So to be a writer, an African woman writer, not just in Africa, but in a small town outside a small city in a small country in Africa—to be Bessie Head and to overcome everything that was thrown her way, and still produce the magic that she did—is a feat worth celebrating from the mountaintops. Some of the people she reached out to for intellectual companionship simply dismissed her as peripheral. The industry took advantage of her solitude and remoteness to rob her. Despite her unquestionable genius, she worked twice as hard for half as much opportunity as her white and male contemporaries. She worked twice as hard and didn't even get half as far.

Today the literary scene has changed considerably, but the relationship between the African woman writer and the core of publishing remains complex. Some room has opened, but only for a certain type of writer—ideally an urbane fiction-writer from the handful of countries that have been appointed as spokespeople for the continent's 1 billion-plus inhabitants. Would a novelist writing magical realism about a small village in an obscure country have any more chance of making it in 2020 than in 1976? Unlikely. The sheer strength of will that Bessie Head must have summoned to create a path to success is probably part of what killed her so early. She was Sisyphus, with the weight of the world on her back and nowhere to put it down—until everything finally gave way.

* * *

I am writing this essay as a tribute to a writer that I love, who moved through the world but struggled to fully live in it, and for whom "home" remained elusive throughout her life. Her country of birth chewed her up and spat her out under a barrage of injustice, only to deify her after her death. The place to which she fled subjected her to frequent reminders that she was an outsider and foreign, until the moment she began to make serious progress as a writer. And then, just when she was about to reap the rewards of her hard work, she was gone.

I think a lot about the arc of Bessie Head's life and what it means for writers everywhere. Is there any lesson to be gleaned from someone who gave her entire life to her vocation, even under the glare of one of the harshest political regimes in history? Is there something we can learn from someone who gave her whole heart to her writing, only to die alone and penniless? Was there a point or a purpose—what does this story mean for the belief that everything happens for a reason and that everything has to amount to something?

Writing is a strange calling. Writers are by their very nature outsiders. You have to be extremely comfortable with solitude and being misunderstood, yet it is that compulsion to be seen and understood that makes a person study the contours of language and learn how to use it to cut through the undergrowth of the world. It takes a special form of madness to lock yourself up in a room for twelve to eighteen hours a day, weeks on end, speaking to nobody and committing words to the page in the hopes that, at some point, someone will pick up what you are putting down and feel a sense of resonance. The money is terrible. Acclaim is sparse. No one remains a writer because they think it will make their life easier. Most of the time, it is that compulsion that Orwell identified in his essay "Why I Write". "Writing a book," he said, "is a horrible, exhausting struggle, like a long bout of some painful illness. One would never undertake such a thing if one were not driven on by some demon whom one can neither resist or understand." He must be right, because Head gave everything to her writing, and it gave her nothing in return.

One day, I ask the librarian at the Khama II Museum if he knows where Bessie Head's home is. He drives a short distance out of town, and at first I am confused: we are back on the road between my hotel and the museum. But it turns out that I have been walking past Rain Clouds every day on my way to the museum. It is a small three-room house that might have been spectacular in its day but is now falling behind neighbours who are clearly profiting from Botswana's recent prosperity. The house is occupied by her son Howard's girlfriend, whom he never got round to marrying before he died at the age of 48. Much like Bessie Head's legacy, it is not unkempt—it is a decently appointed village home that speaks to what might have been a glorious past, and is only just evading disrepair.

I get close to the house. I stand by her grave and say a silent prayer for her rest. I touch the typewriter on which she clack-clacked the words that became her magnificent stories. She built a library for the high school in Serowe, but no one can tell me where it is. The lot where she had planted a small community garden is now a supermarket. Howard never had children, so there is no one to leave flowers at their gravesite; the house that she wrote in is just another house in Serowe. The museum is doing a tremendous job, all things considered, of preserving her legacy and her papers; but, while her male contemporaries—many of whom wrote less and less well—went off to fame and fortune, it hurts a little that Head's legacy amounts to these three rooms in this small, rural museum. There is no real sense of closure at the end of this trip, just a sense of the deep injustice that robs the world of its clearest thinkers when we probably need them the most.

Bessie Head was a literary genius of the highest degree—far more compelling a writer than many of her male contemporaries who have found more acclaim in both life and death. It's hard to call her a victim, because she is much better-read than most African women writers of her day, but she is under-appreciated and relatively unseen. Like most African women writers of her day, Head's books are primarily read through the lens of gender, as well as race, but this subconscious separation of the woman writer from the main canon is dishonest. I think again of that African Literature class and I feel some kind of way that her books were not taught in the main section of the class when she was, objectively, superior to many of the writers that we did read.

Finding Hurston's unmarked and untreasured grave renewed Alice Walker's passion for protecting the work and words of women writers. I wish I could categorically say that it did the same for me. I think what I was left with after my pilgrimage to Serowe was a renewed commitment to give Head to as many readers as possible. I went back to Nairobi and wrote the essay, and it was well received; later I returned to Gaborone for the second edition of their literature festival as kind of a tribute to her legacy. But something has happened to the restlessness that reading *A Question of Power* first triggered in my spirit. Through this project I have connected with Alice Walker, a tremendous gift and moment for me as a reader and a writer. She expresses thanks for the essay, and I feel like I have done something to help her in her journey to elevate black women's writing around the world. And I continue to write, because I must.

7

THE AFRICAN IS NOT AT HOME

In April 2015, Mozambican migrant Emmanuel Sithole was callously pursued, overrun and brutally murdered on the streets of Alexandra township in Johannesburg, South Africa. It was, for many, the high watermark of a season of brutality against African foreigners in South Africa—characterised by random armed groups attacking small businesses owned by Somali and Ethiopian migrants and refugees, followed by a crowd of looters taking the stores for all their worth. Sometimes, before the embers have died in the shells of the burnt shops, these attacks prompt remarks from South African politicians and other public figures seemingly in support of some kind of xenophobic action.

The cycle repeated itself again in 2019 and, by the looks of things, is bound to keep happening. While foreigners are the primary targets, South Africans have not been spared the violence. World-renowned musician Yvonne Chaka Chaka tweeted that her daughter's shop had also been damaged in the 2019 melee—she is one of the bestselling African musicians of all time. There's no reason to hope these violent waves will end, unless and until the South African government develops a policy of inclusion that goes to the root of the problem.

After the end of apartheid and the birth of the rainbow state, there was a significant influx of black Africans from other parts of Africa into South Africa, my own country of Kenya chief amongst them. On one hand, the economy in Kenya was tanking at the tail end of the authoritarian regime. Universities had been gutted by the Structural Adjustment Programmes of the 1980s, as well as systematic efforts by the central government to curb their political activism and their influence on young minds. Many lecturers and dissidents were in exile. But because the Kenyan education system had started strong, you had a whole generation of people with a high level of formal education who could not stay in Kenya and still have the opportunities they felt they deserved. First, thousands went to the UK and the US; then, to South Africa. After the end of apartheid, many Kenyans joined South African universities as full fee-paying students and then stayed to work.

Kenyans were not the only ones headed for the rainbow nation. Ethiopian and Somali refugees established shops and trading outlets in informal settlements and were able to use significant transnational networks to stock them. Both of those countries have large diaspora populations because of the conflict and oppression back home, and the thin sliver of advantage that this offers is a large diaspora network of mutual aid. All of these structural factors have encouraged outsiders to establish themselves in South Africa.

A lot of Africans forget that South African schools were a frontline for the apartheid regime and its policies. The language policy that banned students from learning in their own languages was what triggered the Soweto uprising of 1976, when at least 176 people were killed as the racist police opened fire on protesting students and their parents. After that massacre, the hitherto covert policy of underfunding black schools became overt. The apartheid education system was designed to punish especially urban blacks, to try and compel them to return to rural areas if they couldn't find menial work in the city. Meanwhile, the regime worked hard to distort what black South Africans thought about the rest of Africa. Anti-black propaganda in textbooks filled South African learners with paranoia about the dark continent, and very few people who came of age through this system would have received an alternative education.

Both these factors go some way towards explaining the contemporary history of misunderstanding and bad feeling between black South Africans and other Africans. To be sure, there is still a lot of black–white racism in South Africa. But there's also a rising wave of xenophobia arguing that black Africans from the rest of the continent are, for example, stealing opportunities from black South Africans, and should return home.

One point at which this friction plays out is in the issuance of visas to travel to South Africa. After a brief honeymoon period following Mandela's release, South Africa imposed one of the strictest visa regimes on the continent, requiring many of the same documents that Western nations request for their tourist visas. But unlike the US or the UK, where you can get a five-year or a one-year visa, for a long time South Africa only issued one-month tourist visas for Kenyans like myself, meaning that each time the applicant wanted to visit, they had to endure the indignity of applying all over again. Appeals from the government in Nairobi eventually had this extended to three months, but still the ritual humiliation persists. Three months of bank statements—stamped. Proof of a detailed, step-by-step itinerary and a pre-paid hotel booking. Often, an official invitation from the South African government. For Kenyans, going to South Africa has become a middle-class endeavour, undermining the Pan-African spirit of solidarity that characterised the struggle against apartheid. South Africa's visa protectionism has done more harm than good in the long run, I think. Protectionism always does.

Much of South Africa looks and feels like many other places in the continent, but—conscious of all of the hurdles I have had to go through—I have often entered South Africa without something that I take with me whenever I visit other parts of Africa: a sense of welcome. For those of us who considered ourselves part of South Africa's anti-apartheid struggle, the ambivalence and silence among South Africa's political leadership around the xenophobic violence of recent years has felt like a betrayal of the solidarity and support that was given during the worst years of apartheid. Only Julius Malema, leader of the Economic Freedom Fighters opposition party, has gone on record as rejecting any equivocation when it comes to stopping attacks on African foreigners. In 2019 Naledi Pandor, Minister for Foreign Affairs, requested the Nigerian government's help in "keeping Nigerians in Nigeria". Former President Thabo Mbeki, who himself spent part of his exile in other African countries, echoed the sentiment. Yet, where would South Africa be if thousands of ANC and PAC exiles had not been welcomed across Africa during the struggle?

Professor Achille Mbembe, himself a Cameroonian migrant in South Africa and one of the foremost scholars of African political science, offered these words as a sort of beacon of reason in the chaos of xenophobic violence in 2015: "Finally, one word about 'foreigners' and 'migrants'. No African is a foreigner in Africa! No African is a migrant in Africa! Africa is where we all belong, notwithstanding the foolishness of our boundaries. No amount of national-chauvinism will erase this."

Mbembe's words struck a chord with many Africans and were repeated and even turned into memes as observers tried to craft an anti-xenophobia logic. The instinct was right, powerful and necessary, but flawed and unrepresentative of the reality of life in Africa for many Africans. Africans are not at home everywhere in Africa. We are just as un-homed and othered here—as migrants, refugees, internally displaced persons—as we are anywhere else, a fact that is important to recognise if we are to move away from empty platitudes about Pan-African solidarity and to actually start building just and equitable societies. And to do that, we need to take a hard look at where these tendencies to other and attack our fellow Africans have come from.

* * *

When I think about Pan-Africanism, I often think about one of my favourite passages in Nelson Mandela's autobiography *Long Walk to Freedom*: the section where he describes being smuggled out of South Africa to visit a series of African countries, in search of support for the armed struggle back home. Over a number of months, Mandela received travel documents from Tanzania and Ethiopia, journeyed to thirteen countries and met with leaders from another four. The material support for the ANC and uMkhonto we Sizwe was significant, but so too was personal support for Mandela and his entourage. For example, Sékou Touré, then president of Guinea, heard that the men were low on funds after so much travel, and sent two large suitcases of money for their personal use. It was Guinean money, and not much outside the country, but enough to tide them over until their next destination.

This short sequence has replayed in my mind periodically after the rashes of xenophobic attacks in South Africa. To me, it raises questions about a combination of moral and political obligations that are unique in the post-colonial/post-apartheid state. Africans do owe each other some special consideration when it comes to migration or mobility, but why exactly? Is it simply because we are black? Is it because of a shared history of oppression and fights for liberation? Or because we share this continent?

It seems to me that part of the tension raised by these questions comes from the incomplete process of decolonisation, particularly in former settler colonies like Kenya and South Africa. Many of these xenophobic attacks in South Africa have centred on the Central Business Districts (CBDs) of large towns like Johannesburg and Cape Town; the CBDs were formerly the showpieces of apartheid's illusion of prosperity, but are today somewhat abandoned and falling into disrepair. This cycle of neglect and violence echoes a familiar pattern faced by many former settler colonies in Africa.

As in other British settler colonies like Kenya or Zimbabwe, the CBD in South African cities was a historical epicentre for colonial and racial violence. In fact, colonial Nairobi's apartheid legal structure borrowed directly from South Africa, declaring that the CBD was "the natural domain for the European" and that non-Europeans could only be present with explicit permission from their European "master". It was here that the dreaded pass laws, which punished Africans for being in the city without documentation signed off by their European "master", were most heavily enforced. In the townships and reserves, apartheid focused on engendering fear and enforcing cantonment, creating a pool of labour for white-run farms and industries. In the CBD, apartheid focused on restricting freedom of movement and association through arbitrary arrests and detentions and violent policing, to maintain an enclave of white prosperity. In his memoir, Mandela writes about the many people in Johannesburg's Central Business District who refused to rent him offices for his legal practice: the success of the CBD was predicated precisely on the exclusion and ritual humiliation of black people.

The CBD in Johannesburg—like those in Nairobi and elsewhere—was abandoned after independence, and there was a mass exodus to nearby, newly built suburbs. This echoes the experience of US cities like Detroit and Cleveland, where formerly prosperous city centres have crumbled because that prosperity could not survive desegregation. They had flourished precisely because restricting the movement, association and occupation of non-white residents meant that economic resources could be focused on the white population, while the non-white economic underclass could be effectively exploited by keeping it afraid.

Urban planners call the exodus after desegregation or independence "white flight": once white people, who formerly represented the main tax base in an urban centre, leave for racially homogenous suburbs, cities shift their planning focus to those suburbs and deprive the formerly prosperous CBD of key resources. In South Africa, the rise of Sandton and Rosebank in Gauteng comes at the expense of the Johannesburg CBD area, as the resulting resource vacuum contributes to the CBD's decay, including an uptick in crime. The deterioration of what used to be a symbol of national prosperity then becomes associated with the idea that black people are spoilers who cannot govern effectively. This further drives the exodus, as wealthier non-white communities also abandon the CBD; in extreme cases as in Johannesburg, property values and social services collapse completely.

It makes sense that the Central Business Districts would be a primary site for xenophobic violence in South Africa. The transformation of the settler colony's CBD in the post-colonial state is always accompanied by violence that replicates the contours of colonial violence. I have written elsewhere about how the historical racial violence of Nairobi's CBD is still regularly meted out against women, because in Nairobi African women were not allowed to live in the CBD until the sunset years of the colony. Women who defied this rule were all labelled prostitutes—some were, many were not—and were punished for that. Today, when women are victims of violence in the CBD, it is telling that most are accused of behaving "indecently", the victims routinely called prostitutes, and of intruding on a historically male-dominated space.

In South Africa, the focus of violence has been on foreigners occupying the vacuum created by the retreat of the state, because they are portrayed as having interrupted the black succession of a prosperous CBD, and having caused the deterioration of the space. The exclusion of black South Africans from the CBD was supposed to have ended after the fall of apartheid, the argument goes; instead a new type of foreigner is now standing between the attackers and that illusory space. The same violence that treated black South Africans as intruders in a "naturally white" space, is today visited on "intruding" foreigners. This is the argument that policy-makers subscribe to when they imply that excluding foreigners from South Africa will resolve xenophobia.

Of course all this is illusion. Excluding foreigners who are working and contributing to the economy will not resolve the broader economic issues; it may compound them. A state may claim that it wants to punish criminals—South African or otherwise—for crimes, but excluding migrants wholesale will not resolve the policy failures that are stalling South Africa's decolonisation process. Immigrants did not cause the decay of Johannesburg's CBD. It has happened because cities mistakenly believe that the illusory prosperity of the CBD will somehow sustain itself after desegregation—when, in fact, even more resources are needed for an actively managed post-colonial transition. The poor and immigrants, documented or undocumented, occupy the spaces that open up when urban planning does not decolonise the city properly.

Violence is embedded in the DNA of the postcolonial CBD. To move away from it, an administration must pay systematic attention to the resource gaps created by white flight at independence. The fact that cities like Nairobi and Harare have survived their white flight while Johannesburg struggles is testament to how pervasive and insidious apartheid was in South Africa. The scale of the shift needed is immense, and its aftermath will be too. And while observations about the post-colonial CBD do not speak to all of the social issues around xenophobia in South

Africa, they do hint at another set of questions—including why the economic system sees black foreigners as a threat, while white foreigners are seen as "investors", regardless of how many resources they bring to the table and the points at which they enter the economy. There is a legacy of racial hierarchies there that must be addressed much more comprehensively than simply declaring all foreigners must leave.

* * *

South Africa's fractured relationship with its foreign African population is neither unusual nor atypical in Africa. Consider Mauritania's treatment of its non-Arab population; Egypt's treatment of its ethnically Sudanese population; caste hierarchies in the Indian Ocean islands—the list goes on. I have seen this first-hand in Kenya through the lower status of ethnic Somalis there, both Somali-born and Kenyan-born. In this case, as in all others, the legacy of colonialism has much to answer for in today's hostilities and tensions with the African 'Other'.

Even though historians assert that the Somali arrived in East Africa before Bantu and Nilotic groups, Somalis are today treated as unwanted foreigners and second-class citizens in both Kenya and Ethiopia, not to mention facing the threat of general violence in much of Somalia. Capitalism and consumerism only aggravate underlying tensions, as the profit motive and threats created by economic precariousness distort ethnic and political identities. Ethnic identities that are supposed to be a source of belonging and orientation become conduits for accumulation and even violence, particularly where all other systems fail. When everything else becomes random and unpredictable, religion and ethnicity become the North Star for communities all over the world.

Somali Kenyans doubly suffer, from the tribalism in Kenya's public sphere and from the complications of being a visible minority in a world where "blackness" is itself a variable and malleable construct. In fact the Somali identity is an excellent example of how European colonisation created a category, infused it with politically expedient meaning at the expense of its broader social and economic context, and then left. Kenya's Somali community is transnational and highly fluid. Cross-border migrations between Kenya, Somalia and Ethiopia are historical and common. We should all be in awe of the many ways Somali cultural identity has transcended geographical lines, survived trying historical events, and acutely demonstrated how futile and ultimately meaningless state-based identities can be. Instead, Somalis in Kenya are perpetually othered—foreigners and migrants in their own homes. This anti-black racism now cuts both ways, with some members of the Somali community referring to non-Cushitic Africans with the derogatory *nywele ngumu*—hard hair.

Partly, the un-homing of Somalis in Kenya is due to Kenya's own history of tension with her indigenous Somali population, and residual complications of colonialism rarely contended with in simplified history book narratives. Although today we blithely accept that Kenya was a British colony, colonialism was not a uniform process across the country. Resistance happened, with varying degrees of success—from the coastal city-states that were never officially colonised, to the internment of Nandi and Kikuyu communities in concentration camps, to the Somali resistance in the Northern Frontier District.

In the sixty-odd years that Britain declared itself sovereign over "Kenya", and for the majority of the fifty years that Kenya has been independent, the area formerly known as the NFD has been contested territory. The rebellion there, and its mismanagement by both the colonial and independence governments, has left a legacy of mutual suspicion between the Somali community and the state, as well as punitive underdevelopment. The average

Kenyan doesn't study this part of the country's history, instead collapsing into government-propagated tropes that perpetuate the divide-and rule tradition of governance in Kenya.

For the most part, Somali resistance to colonisation followed clan lines amongst the majority pastoralist population, while the sedentary communities in Kisimayu and the hinterland faced pressure from Ethiopian expansionism that left them open to collaborating with the Europeans. So while much of the Somali community resisted European colonisation all the way through the colonial experiment, a significant portion worked to navigate it, including the Herti of the Ogaden Somalis. These collaborators were rewarded with government positions and opportunities; but, given the racist apartheid state, adjustments had to be made.

Thus, in Kenya's first two censuses in 1948 and 1962, the African population is recorded as divided between the "Native and Somali population", creating a legal distinction between Somalis and other black communities in the colony. Members of the Somali community successfully lobbied the colonial administration to count them as Asians, meaning they would be liable to pay more tax, but would be exempt from the violent Native Registration laws that were the cornerstone of the forced labour and violent reprisal system. These fractures persist within the Somali community today, and when the post-colonial state in Kenya embraced rather than rejected the repressive techniques of the colonial state, oppression of the Somali majority was fully accepted as Kenyan state practice. Every administration in independent Kenya has mounted some kind of violent police or military campaign in the Somali-majority areas of the country.

The duality of this un-homing of Somalis in Kenya is also a consequence of the long-running conflict in Somalia. The transnational nature of the Somali identity—with families and clans spread across international borders—is often framed as a security threat, but there are similarly divided communities along every last one of Kenya's borders, because Kenya's borders are an illogical colonial relic. Since the 1989 conflict broke out, Kenya has had one of the largest refugee communities in the world—until 2016, the largest refugee camp in Africa, and the fourth largest in the world. The vast majority of these refugees are hosted at the Dadaab and Kakuma refugee camps. For many Kenyans, the Somali identity has become inseparable from the refugee identity, even though Kenya hosts refugees of thirty-two different nationalities, and has a sizeable native Somali population.

And so the Somali identity in Kenya exists across these under-lying fissures, in some ways unchanged over millennia, but un-homed by history and contemporary governance strategies that perpetually frame Somalis as "other", in contrast to a schizo-phrenic and itself deeply fractured core.

In April 2015, Garissa University College, the first institution of higher learning ever built in all of what used to be the North Eastern Province in Kenya, was brutally attacked by Al Shabaab militias. The siege lasted for hours, facilitated by the many tacti-cal errors of a systemically corrupt law enforcement apparatus. Almost 150 students at the university were confirmed dead, and around eighty people were injured. The government responded to the siege by threatening to close the nearby Dadaab refugee camp (even though many of the attackers identified were Kenyan), imposing a strict and harshly enforced curfew in Garissa town, and enacting punitive measures against Somali citizens and refugees in Nairobi.

In fact, Collective punishment is perhaps the most brutal face of the un-homing of Kenyan Somalis and Somalis in Kenya. It is neither new nor surprising. After the terror attack at Westgate shopping mall in Nairobi, again in 2015, the government issued a directive that forced all refugees back to camps. A "security operation" in the city rounded up Somali refugees, and Somalis with Kenyan citizenship who were not able to pay bribes demanded by police officers. They were taken to Kasarani, the city's largest stadium. Many were held for days. One woman's infant, who had been at home unsupervised during the raid, died while the mother was in detention.

Almost exactly thirty years earlier, in response to the Shifta rebellion in the region, the Kenyatta government massacred almost 5,000 ethnically Somali Kenyans at the Wagalla Airstrip near Wajir. The country's Truth and Reconciliation Committee, formed after the 2008 post-election violence, recognised this as the worst human rights violation in the country's history. Even though the massacre is a matter of public record, the government only issued a formal apology for the massacre in 2015.

This physical violence is the culmination of a more insidious systemic violence that otherises Somalis in Kenya daily: in ethno-chauvinist discourse, in derogatory remarks or representations in popular culture, in economic and political marginalisation. Government rhetoric around the terror attacks has only exacerbated it, increasing incidences of "jokingly" accusing Somalis of belonging to Al Shabaab. For Somali refugees, it has meant a dramatic contraction of the protection space available in the country—that margin for empathy and acceptance that refugees need in order to feel safe after their flight. For Kenyan-born Somalis, it means a presumption of foreignness until proven otherwise.

South Africa is everything Kenya could have been, had the settler colonialists of Kenya had their way. Much of the legal architecture that built the colonial state in Kenya was borrowed from apartheid South Africa. For example, the Native Registration Ordinance, which compelled every African man over the age of 16 to carry a pass around his neck containing all his biometric details, including fingerprints—this was copied from the South African pass law. That 1915 legislation gave any white person in the territory the authority to summarily arrest, detain and punish any person in breach of the law. It was the backbone of the forced labour system and the racial violence imposed on the colonised population. In Kenya, the Native Registration Ordinance was repealed by 1948 when it became clear that the colony would not survive in its current form, but the runt of the pass still survives in the form of the national ID. There's a sense, when you read Kenyan and South African history closely, that Zimbabwe was South Africa one degree removed, and Kenya two. This is what the colonisers had in mind for us. Can we really be surprised that Africans across the continent seem unable to break free of the instinct to police, otherise and exclude one another?

* * *

As in other African countries, the South African liberation struggle is deeply embedded in Kenya's political psyche, as a rare moment of Pan-African solidarity from a country with a reputation for ducking out of Africa's more complex political challenges. African Socialism, official Kenyan economic policy from 1963, was actually a decision to be brazenly capitalist except when it suited power, and when Africa became a major front in the global economic battle between capitalism and socialism, Kenya simply opted out. The great exception was when it came to the struggle against apartheid: an unusual time when national policy stood for something bigger than economic and political survival.

Probably every generation of Africans up to the 1990s has a liberation struggle that they identify as their own. In the 1950s, Ghana led the way with independence, while in the 1960s there was a whole wave of countries earning their freedom. In the 1970s, all attention was on the Portuguese colonies, which were fighting against the fascist regime; while the 1980s were dominated by Namibia and Zimbabwe. By the 1990s, only South Africa was left, and so I think African millennials identify strongly with that struggle as part of their own history. *Free Nelson Mandela and all political prisoners* was our cry too.

THE AFRICAN IS NOT AT HOME

The televised release of Nelson Mandela from Robben Island is one of the first political events that I remember being conscious of; even though I wasn't a teenager yet, I cried when he won the election four years later. When we were in school, we watched the musical *Sarafina*, singing along to the music while we cried as the movie showed how primary- and high-school-age students were tortured in the name of preserving the system. For us, our protests, marches and boycotts were part and parcel of the struggle against apartheid, and so Mandela's subsequent release and the fall of the apartheid regime was not a South African victory. It was a victory for all of us.

This is a sentiment familiar across the continent, perhaps even more so in countries like Ethiopia or Tanzania that were actually active in their solidarity with the South African resistance. Zambia and Tanzania hosted a shadow majority-rule government formed by South African dissidents. Ethiopia and Tanzania gave Mandela those false travel documents that allowed him to solicit support for the movement abroad. Politicians from the frontline states of Mozambique, Zambia and Angola were actually assassinated by the apartheid South African secret service. Africa walked the long anti-apartheid walk with South Africa, and was punished for it; you could say this is why people wanted to taste the victories too.

I think this is what makes it so difficult for me to be at peace with anti-black racism between different groups of Africans. Countries do not have a political obligation to accept everyone who tries to enter their territory, simply because those countries once helped in their political struggle. But we feel like there is a moral obligation of reciprocity and interconnectedness that at least demands policy-makers interrogate their responses to crises of xenophobia. It's not just a question of debt, but a symbol of a deeper inter-connectedness that is one of the few things of value that one poor country can give to another. What would have happened if the shoe had been on the other foot? The great tragedy is that we now have at least two generations that do not remember or believe in the promise of transnational liberation solidarity on the continent.

In *Long Walk to Freedom*, Mandela himself wrote, "Many people have painted an idealistic picture of the egalitarian nature of African society, and while in general I agree with this portrait, the fact is Africans do not always treat each other as equals." While ordinary Kenyans felt themselves part of the South African liberation struggle, their independent governments were determined to quietly provide support for the apartheid regime. While, on paper, the authoritarian regimes of Jomo Kenyatta and Daniel Toroitich arap Moi were in solidarity with the rest of the African continent against apartheid, in practice, both were reluctant to officially criticise the apartheid regime. Kenya continued to trade with South Africa throughout the apartheid era, and developed a reputation for abstaining or remaining neutral on matters of moral urgency—forgetting that, if you are neutral in the face of oppression, then you have chosen the side of the oppressor. Pan-Africanism is a worthy ideal; but we should not pretend it has always been a reality.

* * *

The idea of Africans universally at home in Africa rightly challenges the idea that identity—national, ethnic, or religious—can be a basis for exclusion of Africans in Africa. It is an idea that gave the Pan-Africanists the united front they needed against the yet more unified colonial identity and its divide-and-rule tactics. It's a form of reclamation: the European created the identity of the "African Negro" and populated it, but the anti-colonial movement negated the content of that definition, even if they retained the politically expedient idea of a single identity. Many of the best-known anti-colonial writers and thinkers—Cabral,

Biko, Sankara—therefore refer to "The African" or "Blacks", even if they give this identity a positive spin.

Appealing to a universal African identity today, as Mbembe did in his retort to South Africa's xenophobic streak, is a great act of resistance to the creeping Europeanisation of African governments' policies on mobility and migration, most recently shaped by Islamophobia. Many countries in Africa are either majority-Muslim or have a significant Muslim minority, and one immediate outcome of these policies has been the fragmentation of previously united societies. It would be useful and even wonderful to have a single African identity that ties us all together through complexities like this. But crafting such an identity would require deliberate social and political choices that I think some people don't want to make. For one, it would involve deconstructing the colonial state completely, and too many Africans are still feeding off that carcass.

There's another dimension to the problem, too: casually distilling African identity in this way irrevocably binds it to something external, and this is usually land. It becomes difficult to separate the idea that human beings come from somewhere, and the idea that human beings *must only* be from that somewhere. This might provide comfort in the short term, but in the long term it feeds into efforts to corral people into different corners of the world, and it makes transnational movement a privilege of the very rich. Perversely, it gives credence to cries of "Africans go home", the xenophobia that many people of African descent struggle with around the world. It suggests that a person can never "leave" Africa—the biological fact of our blackness means that we take Africa with us wherever we go. And again this has different implications for different people. Can Somali migrants ever be Swedish, or will they always be African? How do we reconcile the contradictions of intersectionality when one is primarily a bureaucractic identity and the other is a political one?

How many generations do communities have to go through before they can belong to the new societies that they enter? This version of Pan-Africanism risks overlooking the fact that embedded in the concept of home is a notion of choice.

The reality is that, like any other continent, Africa is a complex and fragmented place. Africans are just as capable of otherisation as people from any part of the world, and just as capable of resorting to dramatic violence in its service. Ideally, Pan-Africanism should be an ideological safeguard against this structural violence, but today's Pan-Africanism as praxis is an ethically compromised ideology that even facilitates this un-homing. In fact, the tendency to over- or under-state our African capacity for violence is dehumanising, because it excuses us from the complexities of human nature. It says we are different, not because of active choices we make or outcomes we will, but because of who we are—a deeply flawed proposition that allows political leaders especially to collapse into empty platitudes instead of having to confront the realities of our complicated societies.

Pan-African solidarity is a wonderful political ideal, but it can't be based on glossing over the violence that we inflict upon each other, or at the expense of addressing the communal traumas that Africans have suffered, specifically minority groups. Hundreds of Africans continue to dare death, crossing the Sahara and the active war zone in Libya, only to meet their untimely end in the Mediterranean. This should remind us all that un-homing of Africans not only persists but drives individuals to increasingly desperate methods of seeking home. Economic un-homing—denying individuals opportunities to carve out a basic livelihood—is just as disastrous as social or political un-homing, especially in a society where wealth or property are a barrier to other opportunities or forms of social access, like education or marriage. Ego and greed by African leaders since 2016 have driven hundreds of thousands of Burundians and South Sudanese into refugee camps, where they have consequently died from preventable diseases or further attacks. That unidentifiable quality that makes somewhere home—peace, settledness, regularity—has been pried violently from them by fellow Africans.

The truth is that millions of Africans are foreigners and migrants in Africa, un-homed by power and abandoned to physical or structural violence. In fact, xenophobia seems to be an inevitable by-product of the contemporary, capitalist state everywhere. It is a consequence of a political system that says you need either money or autochthony to belong, rather than looking at each individual as wholly human, with the ability to contribute. As resources seem to have become increasingly scarce, identity—ethnic, religious, national—has become a basis for determining who can get a piece of the pie. Contestation—structural or physical—becomes inevitable, and xenophobia is one manifestation of this. It isn't an African phenomenon, but neither is it European or American, and it cannot be resolved by well-meaning but ill-informed appeals to a constructed supra-identity.

I like the idea of a Pan-African identity, but it should be grounded in the reality on the continent today, and guided by a shared belief in our humanity. I dream of a Pan-Africanism that is pulling towards something, instead of merely covering up or obfuscating very real and dangerous failures. The solution to this wave of violence against Africans in Africa should be premised on remaking the African state. Do we need new forms of political organisation? Maybe. But we can't, in our rush to get to a supranational utopia, accelerate over the problems created by the political decision to embrace the capitalist state.

For now, we should reject the current trend towards systems that can only exist on the basis of unchecked accumulation by the few. African countries should stop fighting other people's wars—reject international engagements or interventions that encourage un-homing of local populations based on other countries' problems. Pan-Africanism was born of people who believed strongly in the power of the grassroots; that liberation for Africa had to start with those who bore the heaviest burdens of oppression. To be at home, we need societies that are consumed with addressing the needs of the most vulnerable, providing those amenities and supports—the rights—that those of us with more often take for granted. Safety. Adequate healthcare. Meaningful education. A place to lay down at the end of the day. We're not there yet.

By definition, a foreigner is a person who lacks some fundamental right to make claims on the territory in which they are foreign. Today, too many Africans are unable to make these claims of their own countries. Too many Africans are still not at home in Africa.

8

PERIODIC OFFERINGS TO THE VISA GODS

I am fuming. I am sitting on a pavement in a mall in an affluent suburb of Nairobi shaking with anger; a gentle tremble that eventually spills over into a wave of tears. I haven't cried in months and the humiliation that comes from doing it in public only brings on more tears.

The man on the other end of the line has just hung up on me. Throughout the conversation, I was unable to get in a word edgewise as he yelled his invectives and levelled his unfounded accusations. He was a consular officer at a South American embassy in Nairobi, where I had just deposited my visa application and gone to the bank in order to pay the required fee. Apparently, one of the staff members had complained that someone had been rude to them and, as best as I can put together, he was calling every single person that had applied for a visa that day and cancelling all their applications. There was no appeal process or questioning—just an angry call letting you know of the decision.

It is one week to the day before I am scheduled to fly. This is more than just an inconvenience—I stand to lose almost $800, or half a month's wages. Suddenly, I am no longer confused; I am angry, breathing heavily, grinding my teeth—and if my spirit could talk it would be a loud, deep protracted growl, like the grind of a drill going through a concrete wall. I have listened to the man speak slowly while trying not to grind my teeth. I do what many people are doing when they are angry: I tweet, and I post on Facebook. I am nobody, there is no string to be pulled that I know of. He has made his decision and I must live with it.

As I drive the forty-five minutes back to my office, I catch myself in the subtle act of qualifying why I am a good migrant and why what the consul did is fundamentally unfair. I am playing the game. I am qualifying my humanity on the basis of hurdles of worthiness put in place by governments to slow down black and brown bodies racing towards the opportunity that these countries believe they offer. "Do you know who I am?" is my first instinct, and I act on it, but I quickly catch myself thinking: does it matter? What if I am a nobody? What if I am just an ordinary young woman with no antecedents to recommend herself to another country, and I just want to go there? Why must I crouch low and bow subserviently to be considered worthy to enter? Why must I play the game?

* * *

Visas are a cruel and unusual invention. They are a reminder of the humans' near-infinite capacity to invent things out of thin air and then reorder their lives completely around it, including their measure of the value of human life. Theoretically, a visa is a small piece of paper that goes into your passport to tell the immigration official that you are good and deserve to enter. But in practice, the documents have become loaded with all the politics of a rapidly securitising, racist and violent world. The visa is a stamp of authority and approval. The visa is a means of control. The visa is a tool for humiliation. The visa is a document that reminds you—and especially all of us unwashed masses of the global South—that we are fundamentally unwanted in the West, and this flimsy document is all that stands between us and summary ejection. The visa is a power play, a cash grab, and a half-assed invitation to enter but not belong.

People with powerful passports often miss why the rest of us complain about visas. They think that what we are objecting to is the complex and weighty bureaucracy that surrounds them; and that if the process was just made more efficient, it would be fine. But visas are loaded with ritual humiliations and demands for obeisance that are designed to remind the applicant that they are lesser. For single Nigerian women to travel to Thailand, they must provide a letter from their father authorising their trip. For Kenyans to enter Canada, they must provide proof of wealth. Then there are the interviews: an intricate dance where you don't want to seem too subservient, but you might miss out on your visa if you aren't subservient enough. The entire edifice is built to remind people of their place in the constructed hierarchies of the world.

I tried to find the history of visas for this essay but the information in the public domain is scarce. All I can say for certain is that, until the second half of the twentieth century, most people could travel without a passport, let alone a little piece of paper giving you permission to enter a specific country. The case of Kenya and the UK is instructive. Before 1888, Kenyans were in Kenya and British people were in the UK. Some missionaries came over uninvited and established missionary schools in small towns, first along the coast, then in the hinterland. Then some settlers decided to build a railway line to connect Uganda to the coast. They brought over thousands of Indian men who had built a similar railway back home as indentured labourers. These railway-builders were also uninvited, although they did carry documents from their government to introduce themselves to each other. In 1897, the colony of Kenya was declared, and suddenly white British people could enter and leave the territory nearly at will.

In 1915 the colonial administration introduced rules that made it impossible for an African man over the age of 16 to move through the territory without the permission of his white employer. But these rules fuelled waves and waves of armed resistance that never quite stopped until independence in 1963. By this time, educated Africans were able to travel to the UK if they could afford it—some went there to study, others went to agitate for independence. Kenya, for example, had a strong delegation at the 1945 Pan-African Congress in Manchester, including the country's soon-to-be first president Jomo Kenyatta. Between 1963 and 1997, Kenyans could travel to the UK without a visa as part of the Commonwealth. Given how much death and upheaval British colonisation had created, this seems logical.

But from 1989 to 1997, the Kenyan economy began to collapse as the authoritarian regime refused to transition to a properly, democratically elected government. Millions of Kenyans left the country, and many headed to the UK. A number of these Kenyans were descendants of the Indians who had built the railway, who were offered special routes to British citizenship because their ancestors had been brought to East Africa by force.

Between 1997 and 2017, the UK visa regime has changed dramatically. Not only are visas granting entry to the United Kingdom prohibitively expensive, they are also bureaucratically complicated. Applicants must provide three months of bank statements, prove that they own property in their home country, give a reason for their visit and proof of where they will be staying when they get there, offer detailed itineraries and other invasive personal details. More importantly, the UK government has a policy of making the Home Office—the government department that issues visas—pay for itself. This means that the visa regime has also become a money-making venture, with more and more costs tagged onto even simple visitor visas, even if there is no guarantee that the application will be successful.

The visa regime is conceived as the frontline defence in expressing countries' fears of conquest and invasion, in many cases from the same territories that these powers spent the previous century conquering and invading.

But the visa has become more than just a practical bureaucratic barrier. Visas force us all to play into a world where we can say, think or do racist and classist things, without ever having to name the thing behind the thing. This has become another face of the racial violence that countries inflict on each other—a sort of offering to gods of division, segregation and exclusion, who require periodic appeasement. Complex requirements are inflicted wholesale on relatively poor countries, not because they perform a specific function other than to raise money for the dominant country, but to remind the poorer country that its people are poor and unwelcome. There are no individuals before the visa gods.

I often get into this argument with people who say, "How else can we prevent fraud?" and I think that this is entirely missing the point. You could, in theory, run a visa regime without charging a single cent. You could put in place the same level of scrutiny and demands for documentation without charging a single cent—chalk it up as a necessary public expense. But the fact that many wealthy countries are charging a fortune to residents of poor countries, just to subject citizens of the latter to these opaque rites of humiliation, speaks to the philosophy of race embedded within the system. Add to this the fact that these onerous fees are charged before the applicant knows what the outcome of their application will be, and you see the current visa regime, in the Schengen zone and beyond, for what it is: a blatant cash-grab and resource transfer from poorer to wealthier countries. The point is not just to continue to screen outsiders—it is to humiliate groups and keep them in their place, by any means necessary.

The data backs up this argument, showing that visas are pre-configured for discrimination. A 2019 study of Canadian immigration data found that three of every four African students had had their student visa applications rejected, and that students from African countries were far more likely to experience this than those from any other region. The global average for rejection of Canadian student visas is only 39 per cent. Somalia and Mozambique had the highest level of rejections—100 per cent of all Canadian student visa applications. Considering that each student visa application costs $160 in application fees and another $100 to provide biometrics, the Canadian government is raking in millions worldwide from African student visa applications that it knows it is going to reject.

What the current global visa regime says is that everyone from a poor country is a suspect in immigration fraud until proven otherwise. The converse argument is almost never made, even when there is significant evidence to the contrary. There are, for example, a number of white Westerners working in African countries on tourist visas, people who overstay visas or hop in and out of the country. In 2019, the Thai government prohibited "beg-packing", where white backpackers travel throughout South East Asia, begging well-wishers for support to keep their adventure going. These are things that African travellers can never do; even people on work permits are under the heaviest scrutiny. Once, on a train from Vienna to Geneva while I was a student, my friend and I were the only two black people in a full train car. And we were the only two who were asked to produce our passports to the ticket inspector—in violation of EU free movement protocols.

This is why I didn't want to play the game when I was unfairly victimised by the consul in Nairobi. My instinct was to scream from the mountaintops about how I was a "good" migrant and didn't deserve to be treated in this way; but that would just reify the idea that black and brown people must fulfil some opaque normative standard in order to gain admission. The point isn't that the system is bad at separating "good" visitors from "bad". The point is that the system is inherently built for exclusion, profiteering and petty tyranny. The challenge is, how do we call out the injustices if those who have a measure of privilege—either a platform, or access—don't speak out about it?

At the time of writing this, I still haven't figured out how to do that. I keep coming back to the fact that, if they wanted to, most of the countries that have in place these tyrannical visa regimes could actually make them at the very least more afford-able, and if not more affordable, at least more transparent. But that would require a significant amount of solidarity and scrutiny from the citizens of those countries—for them to be willing to see the struggles of people on the other side of the world through a justice lens, rather than through an entitlement lens. People would have to accept that their passport privilege, which exempts them from these visa regimes, is nothing more than an accident of birth. But maybe that's why they fight so hard to protect it—because it is in fact built on such fickle ground.

For the visa system to be truly reformed, the vast majority of the world's population would have to accept fundamental equality with people from other parts of the world, a proposition that goes completely against the core propositions of their myths of politi-cal exception. Not many societies are prepared to accept that. And so we will keep moving the cups around, shifting our ranks and orders of presumed goodness or worthiness, but never quite eliminating the systemic inequalities that this ranking creates.

As for me, it turned out that someone within reading dis-tance of my social media had significantly more power than I did, and later that night, I got an email from their Ministry of

Foreign Affairs apologising for the incident and asking me to submit my documents directly to them. I was also invited to meet with the ambassador in Nairobi so that she could apologise and sort the situation out personally. I went to the meeting and spoke candidly and clearly to the three people present—the ambassador, the political consul, and the local staff member who had claimed that she'd been insulted. The latter admitted to all of us that I had not been party to the abuse—that in fact it was the irate gentleman ahead of me in the line who had been out of control. I had made small talk with this man while we waited for the embassy to open, but we were not applying together. The ambassador apologised that I had felt racial discrimination at the embassy. But the consul refused to back down. Neither of them knew that I understood their language and what they were saying to each other—she asked if he would just approve the visa, but he refused because he was offended that I had called him a racist.

In the end, he asked me to apologise in English. I apologised to the ambassador if she felt that my social media posts had given their country a bad name. I told the local staff member that I was sorry she had had a bad day and that I was grateful that she had acknowledged I wasn't part of the reason for it. But I refused to apologise to the consul. Because a person can only bend so low before their back is broken. I asked for my passport back and left.

9

AFRICA FOR BEGINNERS

Achille Mbembe wrote in *On the Postcolony* that "the African human experience constantly appears in the discourse of our times as an experience that can only be understood through a negative interpretation. Africa is never seen as possessing things and attributes [that are] properly part of 'human nature.' Or, when it is, its things and attributes are generally of lesser value, little importance, and poor quality. It is this elementariness and primitiveness that makes Africa the world par excellence of all that is incomplete, mutilated, and unfinished, its history reduced to a series of setbacks of nature in its quest for humankind." Perhaps this is why the Lonely Planet guidebook used to call Nairobi "Africa for Beginners". The implication is that Africa is hard, and you need to start off somewhere easy that won't overwhelm you from the outset.

I find this characterisation hilarious, especially now that I've travelled as much as I have. I love my home town with all of its complications and contradictions. But Nairobi is not easy. Nairobi is good at allowing people to opt out from its eccentricities at the right price. Nairobi is good at making things easy for people who have the right connections and the right bank balances.

Some time ago, I chaired a small academic conference in the UK broadly on the theme of "Nairobi". The professor who asked me to chair it no doubt asked me to do so because I was the only Kenyan he knew at the time—I was also the only African on the entire schedule, but I didn't notice this until the conference was actually underway. Afterward, I was left thinking more about the people who study Africa than about Africa itself.

In a panel of seven academic papers, five were on Kibera or informal settlements in general, and only one did not deal explicitly with a development-style topic. An entire city of almost 4 million inhabitants with a rich and complex history; a microcosm of the entire East African region combining all that is good and terrible about the place and taking it to the next level—but all that researchers seem to see when they look at Nairobi is the slums. What does that say about the people who study African cities? What does that say about what we think is interesting or worth pursuing about the city?

The lenses that we use to process the information we read about a place are not neutral, but actually bend the details to fit our worldview and what we think matters. Bertrand Russell once wrote that "Marco Polo never noticed that Chinese women had tiny feet"—because when he was in China, women were not interesting subjects of inquiry; their feet even less so. Academics like V.Y. Mudimbe and Mahmood Mamdani have wondered in their writings what we can learn about the academy from the way scholars think about Africa. Much of the dominant academic conceptions of the continent is nothing more than a projected image that Europeans have of themselves, continuing a colonial legacy of dichotomising and atomising the African experience through the lens of European institutions.

A lot of this filtering is down to how people define interesting. The unspoken position that something alien or "wrong" is more interesting than what we think is "normal" or "right" shapes how we prioritise objects of study, particularly in political science and international relations. For instance, the perceived poverty of the African urban experience relative to suburban living in Europe and North America. The recurring discussion on failed states and failed markets is another example. A further problem is that we've set up academic inquiry so that the focus is on studying what can be studied, rather than what simply is. And, especially when it comes to African societies, the humanities have been edged out in favour of the sciences and, at a very distant second, the social sciences—meaning that the academy barely has the soft tools needed to make sense of the complexity and multifacetedness of African people or African cities.

So, instead of complex analyses of the relationships between power, institutions and people, we end up with rehashed conjectures on "ethnicity" or "gender" that are neither informative nor, in many cases, that interesting. And instead of considering what possibility lies in the African city as a site of contestation, but also conciliation and social change, we end up with rather essentialist discussions of poverty that imply nothing else of significance happens in these cities.

Poor people are not just their poverty. People who live in slums are not defined by their housing situation. The inability to distinguish between the two leads to a lot of half-truths and half-baked interventions. I think that the average person who lives in an informal settlement would love to have better housing and access to services. But they would also love to maintain some of the cultural and social dynamics that have evolved in the space, including social opportunities that, in a place like Nairobi, are not available anywhere else. Consider that at the time of writing there are around four orchestras in Nairobi: the Nairobi Philharmonic; the orchestras of the upmarket St Mary's and Lenana Schools; and Ghetto Classics, a philanthropic initiative to teach music in the informal settlement of Kayole. When people resist the breaking apart of informal settlements, what is it that they are resisting?

There have been some interesting studies lately about middle- and upper-class Kenyans, but the majority of Kenya's urban population—us working stiffs who walk to work three weeks a month and only have enough petrol money to cover the fourth; we who pay for internet and cable when the salary comes in, but aren't always able to maintain the connection throughout the month—we are less well understood. The stories told about places like Nairobi or Johannesburg intentionally overlook the contributions of the real middle class, instead focusing on the tension between the very rich and the very poor. Yet this dynamic is a big part of what gives a city its character.

So when Lonely Planet calls Nairobi "Africa for Beginners", they're not talking about the street skaters of Majengo or the Somali restaurants of Eastleigh. They're not writing about Gikomba market or the nyama choma restaurants in Kenyatta Market. They are writing about all the upmarket places that have been deliberately packaged to be easy for outsiders, often to the exclusion of locals. They are writing about restaurants that regularly refuse admission to black diners and revellers. They are talking about places that will leave black paying customers standing around idly for almost an hour waiting for service. They are talking about a tourism paradigm that Kenyans call "*sahani za wageni*"—that preserves the best for outsiders, but treats its own like garbage.

Which makes the academic fascination with informal settlements particularly interesting. I often think that researchers are more fascinated by how other people's poverty makes them feel than they are interested in whether their research has any actual utility. Like war correspondents with a taste for blood, being on the frontline of other people's poverty without actually having to live in it gives them a sense of reward or satisfaction. You can tell the difference between a person who is walking in solidarity with the communities they study—someone who learns the language and works hard to understand better the unspoken cultural codes—and a person who is voyeuristically peering into people's struggles for their own ends. If the wealthy parts of the city are Nairobi for beginners, then the informal settlement is its logical opposite: Nairobi for expats, or Nairobi for professionals.

The academic focus on informal settlements generally and Kibera specifically has serious consequences for those who are studied. Kibera is an extremely over-researched community. I used to teach in Kibera, and I always marvelled at how many white people there were walking around in small groups, usually headed up by a black man, and how my students who struggled with high-school English could casually drop social science terminology into conversation. Many of the young people of Kibera have mastered the art of selling their stories to those who pay a good price for them—and who can blame them when they are simply supplying what the market demands? Young, relatively educated men especially seem to find this a viable alternative to crime. But it also compels them to "otherise" their own communities, to pathologise their existence and to dislocate themselves from their day-to-day reality in order to sell convincing stories. We can only wait and see what impact this will have on the communities over time.

I think "Africa for Beginners" is the most misguided way of describing Nairobi. My city is a complicated place that will love you and hate you in equal measure, at the same time, with the same intensity. A place where you can have torrential rain destroy your roof while your taps run dry. It is, just like any city, a place riddled with the violences and contradictions of unexpected growth. We love to romanticise cities but the truth is, we really don't understand how to make them work properly for everyone.

Every city has its bright side and its dark side, and sometimes the path to the one is through the other. Nairobi is layers of culture and history colliding in crude and unexpected ways. Some statistics say that half or even two thirds of the world's population will be living in cities by 2030. Nairobi is a great example of how little we understand of what that will mean.

My experience with the Nairobi conference may well have been a curious coincidence. After all, university departments are often ideological silos where people with similar ideas on how the world works can seek each other out and reinforce their pre-existing notions. And my own deep personal connection to the subject matter was perhaps the antithesis of what social scientists have in mind when they preach "objectivity". Still, would it be too much to ask for people to look at the African city and see more than just poverty?

10

UKABILA

Every five years for almost thirty years, Kenyans have gone to the polls, and every election within that period has rubbed the wounds of a deeply fragmented society raw and open once again. Every action and reaction are met with accusations of tribalism and demands for ethnic loyalty. "We" are not like "them": somehow this thing we can't define, beyond the fact that our fathers—never mothers—gave it to us, is about to divide us in irreparable ways. The vote will ask us to choose, but not along the lines that seem obvious. We will self-divide into three camps: those who vote with the group, those who vote against it and the handful of people who will actually vote according to their own interests. The analysts will swarm and begin their campaign to single out the tribe as the root of all evil, stopping Kenyans from doing anything other than destroying each other completely every five years. Then something completely avoidable but still distressing will happen, we will be horrified, and finally we will shrug and say, "*Ukabila.*"

There are people who have built careers on arguing that ethnicity and race are kissing cousins, but I think that tribalism or ethnicity has an elusiveness and malleability that race can never really aspire to. Both are aspects of identity that suffer the burden of being reorganised and weaponised according to the interests of power. Both have flourished in capitalist political systems where competition, not co-operation, is the central organising principle. But whereas race is tied to a physical or biological trait—no matter how fluidly and changeably that trait is defined—for most people the ethnic group isn't. The thing that gives the tribe or ethnic group its political power is precisely that it is an ever-shifting target, one that insinuates itself completely into the deep state and gives rhyme and reason to practices that would otherwise be unacceptable. It's one of those things that people project so much meaning and symbolism onto, but for many it is nothing more than a shared name, a common hometown, or an obligation to intervene.

I find the idea of tribe fascinating. The word itself is loaded and dripping with violence. Those of us who come from societies where the word "tribe" was imposed have never called ourselves that. It is a word dripping with the disdain of colonising forces for local communities; a desire to give form to the fear of marauding natives running wild. It is all of the contempt and condescension that white settlers felt against the Other. Generally, only societies that have been through the violence of colonisation are put into the taxonomies of tribes. In fact, if the violence of colonisation could be distilled and captured in a single word, that word would be tribe. In themselves the colonisers saw "high societies" and organised politics; in the Other they saw chaotic brutes organised according to indiscernible, inferior clusters that they called the tribe. The term is riddled with the idea that this is something that lesser people do.

Native American communities still use the word to refer to themselves—so do many Kenyans. I think part of this is about the fact that most of us really aren't privy to the full history of violence and contempt that the word carries with it. We see it define something that we haven't ever really thought about systematically, much as most cis people don't think through their gender identities and just use whatever characteristics they find in their society. I think what I think about the politics of the tribe because I study it. I spend hours unpacking how British settlers built an exogenous structure around what was a much more fluid system of identity and belonging, and then reified it with political systems designed to punish and to generate compliance. I am deeply fascinated by the determinism that so many people project onto "tribe", knowing full well that as a heterosexual African woman it is perhaps the one aspect of my identity that I cannot pass on to any children I may have, because those are the rules that the patriarchy settled on. It's one of those things that you can't really explain to an outsider, but those of us who live with it can see it coming from miles away.

Toni Morrison was on to something when she told us that "we do language. That may be the measure of our lives." Or, as we say in Kenya, English came on a boat. The Swahili word for tribe is *lugha* or *kabila*; the former is actually the word for language, and the latter has only really come into popular use because of the nominal form *ukabila* for tribalism. "*Wewe ni kabila gain?*"—What tribe are you?—is something that a lot of Kenyans used to ask each other, but that changed considerably after the 2007 election, because in the wake of the vote that question—whether asked directly or implied by asking for an identity card—was followed by violence. Today, the question is loaded with the weight of this tragedy and, for those of us who witnessed the violence uncomfortably close, is deeply offensive. It is a reminder of the relationships that were ended because former lovers found themselves on opposite sides of the national divide. Which is what makes it amusing when white foreigners in Kenya, attempting to demonstrate their bona fides, ask the question, as if to say, "I know Kenya; I know you guys have tribes." It's a taboo question that says the opposite: reminding those of us who came close to losing everything—because of that last name, that hometown, or that linguistic inflection—that we could be back there again any time.

It's not that there were no ethnic groupings in Kenya before the arrival of the British or Portuguese, and sometimes these hostilities did devolve into violence. But the colonial consolidation or solidification of the tribe was taxonomic violence. Groups that would otherwise consider themselves independent were jumbled together into language families that made no sense, except that they made the territory easier to govern. The Marachi, Bukusu, Maragoli, Isukha, Banyala and about seventeen language groups, many of which are mutually unintelligible, were mangled together as the "Abaluhya", a word that some scholars suggest simply means "people". And the justifications for the categorisations were as random as the categories themselves. Even though some Somali groups were pastoralist and others were sedentary, the colonial myth was that the Somalis were one tribe with many clans; but the same categorisation saw the Kalenjins as distinct ethnic groups. This is what I mean by taxonomic violence: sorting people according to criteria that make no sense to the categorised and only serve the political power of the person doing the categorising. This in part explains why we resist the label tribe. Words have meaning beyond the lexical.

Yet, Kenya being a country of many languages—and many identities embedded in them—there are lots of people who are more comfortable with the word than you would expect. Most Kenyans are not thinking in English, but performing English as translation or a close approximation of the word that we have in mind, in Kiswahili or another language. The average Kenyan doesn't believe that those words carry the weight of prejudice and disdain that the English "tribe" has, almost as if "tribe" is being translated out of context. We use the word without its politics, because in our minds we hear the less violent Swahili or other Kenyan language version. We say "tribe" because no other word has that same baggage—but we don't engage with the baggage. This is a lesson in political etymologies: how the origin of a word and its political use can come to colour it permanently, and how its continued use reflects the politics of the user.

I have to confess, though, I hate tribe's euphemistic cousin—ethnicity—just as much. I think "ethnicity" makes solid something that we who use the language know to be rather fluid and malleable. An ethnic identity is not like a race or a gender identity; it exists almost entirely in the mind. I think ethnicity is more important to the analyst than it is to the analysed—it gives the observer a lens through which they can categorise and process various relationships and connections, but doesn't actually have as much explanatory power as the analysis claims. A proper definition of what these groups are would capture how quickly they change depending on political exigencies, and at the same time how much sway they have on a person's political and social outcomes. Finding a "correct" word for that big family or language or hometown—capturing the essence and complexity of what colonisers and anthropologists have called "tribe" or "ethnicity"—would be no easier than bottling the wind.

That's not to say that ethnicity doesn't matter or have real-world significance. More that it doesn't matter the way people think it matters. As a woman, I grew up with a very specific experience of tribe or ethnicity in Kenya. I inherit it from my father and I lose it as soon as I marry. I can't pass it on to any children, unless they are intentional about carrying it forward. Most of its political implications are distilled to the person's last name and the language they speak, and given and withdrawn at will, so that a female minister who marries outside her tribe is identified with her husband's tribe—until she crosses them. Then, she must "go back to her people".

Are tribalism and racism the same thing? They have the same social function. They are both efforts to define and marginalise. They both reflect the interests of the person who did the categorising more than the interests of the person living within the categories. They both do a tremendous amount of damage when weaponised and politicised. They have both been used as a justification for all forms of social exclusion. But it is possible to opt out of the burden of tribe in a way that it isn't possible to opt out of the complexities of race. A person can learn a language, move town, marry into another big family and evade the worst violence. And that is what makes tribalism even harder to unpack than race, I think. It is whatever the person wielding it wants it to be for their political intentions.

The intensity or fraughtness of ethnicity also varies significantly with the political temperature. Things that would be laughed off or ignored in between election years suddenly become life-or-death debates: having the wrong surname at the wrong place during Kenya's 2007–8 post-election violence left many people dead. In politically tense moments, a person's name and the implications of ethnicity that come with it become critical. What do you do with a thing that isn't until it is, and when it is, consumes everything?

If Kenya is any indication, you struggle. You recognise that this group that is bigger than the family but smaller than the nation is important for many people's social welfare and their ability to survive a complex political and economic situation. But you also know keenly that this lever, which can be turned at a whim to exclude and penalise entire communities, is a pressure valve that power will abuse. You conflate it with numerous other things that make it a catch-all for class, race and even gender. You use it to opt out of accountability for the worst social and economic crimes. You watch the patriarchy use it as a weapon against women and sexual and gender minorities. You watch it become commercialised as an informal savings and lending system. You lose friends and family, because you wake up one day the wrong tribe in your social circle, at a time when "tribe" is being used to tear the nation apart.

* * *

For urban Kenyans, the politics of ethnicity are incredibly fluid. Many of the post-colonial generation who grew up in the city speak multiple languages, because in 1950s and '60s Nairobi kids didn't really grow up speaking either English or Kiswahili. Moving freely between Kikuyu, Luhya, Kamba and the many subgroups of Luhya is what you had to do in order to be able to play. Recalling that tribe or ethnicity doesn't normally correspond to any physical characteristics—that people from different tribes don't necessarily look different—where does the tribe end or begin? Does picking up Kikuyu make one Kikuyu? Is a Kamba kid who picks up Dholuo in order to play with the Luo children in their neighbourhood any less Kamba? Where does ethnicity begin and where does it end?

In English, the word tribe has both Latin and Old French roots, and the dictionary says that it began as a reference to one of the twelve political and ethnic groups that emerged from Jacob's twelve sons in Judeo-Christian theology. The ethnic group is an idea that there is an original kinship connection between people, one that can be traced beyond immediate and extended family to a defined moment in history. The ethnic group is less than a family, but more than a random collection of strangers. It is the belief that if you yank on the thread of connection, you can eventually find an original stitch uniting everyone.

Certainly in the way it is used in the Bible, Koran or Torah, the word tribe isn't as derogatory and loaded as when it is used in English. This raises the question—when did it become something that Those People do? When does a "tribe" become a "nation"? If we flip the gaze back onto Europe, what do these two words reveal about the continent and its people? Both nations and tribes rest on the demands that their members make on each other—loyalty, tolerance, forgiveness, support and other intangible political or social claims. Why is one recognised as a neutral or even desirable political unit, and the other seen as inferior and inherently flawed?

Are tribes primitive? The barbarous origins of the European nation-state—the violence that was the basis for European societies' organisation—suggests that there is nothing inherently inferior or superior about the "nation" versus the "tribe". When we look at the history of criminal punishment in the UK, we see that loyalty to the ideals of the nation-state was built over time through the use and misuse of violence. Trial by ordeal, for example, subjecting people to all kinds of torture in the name of divining justice, only ended in the seventeenth century. The nastiest wars of the twentieth century have all either happened in Europe or had a significant European or Western involvement, whether through weapons sales, proxy interventions or actual soldiers on the ground.

So why do we, the black and brown populations of the world, get to have tribes, while Europe gets nations?

It may be intellectual laziness. Specifically, I think it reflects an unwillingness to do the heavy lifting needed to challenge the thinking that made domination possible. I say this with the full knowledge that anthropology—and, to a lesser extent, sociology and other disciplines—are working to try and change this internally. But there is a specific subset thinking about power and how society organises it that needs the tribe to be more useful than it actually is. It has to function as a substitute for patriarchy, for example, because if it was defined as a product of patriarchy, the people doing the analysing would have to grapple with the presence of patriarchy in their own lives and work. You would have to develop the tools to understand that men need this thing to exist, to enable them to subjugate everyone else.

One of these complex analytical tools would be something allowing us to distinguish between the patriarchal means of such subjugation and the loyalty networks that make life possible in countries where the state has no monopoly on the use of force or the organisation of public life. "Tribe" is used as an justification for powerful men supporting each other in politics and young men organising to create violence, but also for women coming together to launch saving and lending societies—whereas in the West these activities would be separately explained as fraternities, gangs and co-operatives respectively.

The tribe as used in political science has become a euphemism for backwardness and a shorthand for more complex phenomena. There remains in political science a colonial belief that if the Other could just be liberated from his tribe, he could find progress or happiness; if we could just get rid of "tribalism", everything would get better. But is the tribe the natural and inevitable province of the disadvantaged Other, or is it something that people build and use to navigate their historical moment?

Post-coloniality has created some of the tools and arguments needed to put the tribe in its correct place. These writers and thinkers push back against the idea that one system of political organisation is inherently and irrefutably superior to another. Chinua Achebe's *Things Fall Apart* is often lauded as a work of cultural critique, but I would argue that it is also a work of political defence: proposing the idea that loyalty to the tribe should never be all-consuming, but nor should it be rejected wholesale—unless we want a countryside littered with Okonkwos with no clear sense of whether they are coming or going.

I think it's lazy to blame the ethnic group for everything that's wrong with politics in Kenya. We are sexist, classist and struggle with race too. If anything, it is politics—both the history of colonisation and today's winner-takes-all election model—that has ruined the group. What was initially a sociopolitical institution that primarily offered social welfare benefits has now become the focus for negative campaigning and exclusionary politics. Remember that, at the germ, political parties in Kenya flowed naturally from the merger of various ethnic welfare associations, because the colonial government used the tribe as the basis for political organisation, punitive measures and all systems of government. The consolidation of the tribe as the basis for political resistance was a reaction to the use of the tribe as a unit for political oppression. I don't think it was supposed to serve the political functions that have been grafted onto it in independence.

The tribe gave people a sense of orientation and a sense of belonging; that there was some place where, no matter where you went, you could always belong, and people would have to put up with you even if you were rotten to the core. The tribe demanded more than it gave—there were no welfare cheques, there were no consular services. Instead, in exchange for your unfailing commitment to protect and help other members of the group, what you got was the feeling that maybe someday someone would do the same for you. You got a hometown that could never turn you away no matter what you did. You got a language that gave you words for things reflecting the reality of that hometown—like its flora and fauna, which serve a specific cultural function. You got a place where you belonged and that almost no one could take away from you (unless, of course, you were a woman).

With the introduction of modern competitive politics, suddenly that group has found itself in a position to give out rewards. The inaccurate translation of "large tribe" as "nation-state" in the decolonisation process changed its primary function, into acquisition and distribution of state resources. Politicians who had been exposed to Western competitive politics took the reins in many countries, and perhaps sensed that they could maximise personal gain through a combination of public pursuit of politics and private demands for ethnic fealty. The group was never meant to be a unit for large-scale political mobilisation; but in the absence of any other meaningful focal point of organisation, it has become one.

Predictably, a tool being used for a job it was not designed for is failing miserably. In the unchecked pursuit of capitalism, we killed the trade unions, welfare associations and any other institutions that enhance the allocative and redistributive functions of the state in a democracy; and then we wonder why people are willing to die for their tribes. The tribe was the only African institution to be legitimised in the colonisation process, and is the only one that was not, at least in Kenya, delegitimised in the post-colonial era.

It is easy to cry for the abolition of the tribe or ethnic group— I should know, I used to believe in that too. However, after almost a decade of living in countries that think they don't have these groups, I've slowly changed my mind. I would rather see a world where the group was put in proper perspective—as another useful source of identity—and where we leaned into the complexity of all the various forces we are placing in the bucket of "tribe" or "tribalism". The experience of women is a great starting point for beginning this process: what does the tribe look like when your central referent object is not a man, but a woman instead? What structures yield and which ones survive? What things does the tribe fail to protect against—domestic violence, erosion of child welfare—and what does that tell us about the function tribe actually performs?

Maybe we need a new word that captures both the fluidity of the ethnic group and its complex history. We need a word recognising that this thing is just as fluid as it is solid. Something that maybe detaches it from the violent history without erasing its social utility; that acknowledges how it moves across domains, constantly changing yet eerily still the same. Maybe something like "language network"; something that captures what it feels like for those of us who live within it. Maybe we need to work harder at bottling the wind.

In my experience, an ethnic group is just another layer of identity that one has to navigate in order to survive the madness of the world. It is something that I am aware of, but not something that I think about constantly. It is something whose significance crops up in moments of friction, but I try not to give it more explanatory power than it deserves. As a heterosexual woman, I am very conscious that my relationship with my broader ethnic group is contingent on my marital status and my relationship with the family and community I marry into. I recognise that many of the characteristics attributed to it are a product of patriarchy. I don't believe that it is inherent enough in my sense of self for the government to keep putting it on my primary identity card, especially as it continues to be a point of vulnerability and possible violence around election time. *Ukabila* is a projection of constructed identities, a product of the collective imagination of the societies I inhabit; on a practical, day-to-day level, it buffers against some harsh realities that can make life intolerable. For example, to help us make peace with the fact that in the end we all die alone.

11

THIS IS FOR THE COMMUNITY

A few years ago I was looking for an apartment in Nairobi. Anyone who has lived in Nairobi will tell you that house-hunting here is an extreme sport. It's not that there aren't any apartments in the city—in fact there's a glut. It's just that the market is littered with fraud. Fake websites for letting agencies that don't exist. Agents charging a commission on top of a commission for introducing landlords to tenants, and vice versa. The easiest way to find a home in Nairobi without taking on all the extra risk is to put on your sturdiest walking shoes and go door to door from housing complex to housing complex, asking the security guards if there are any vacant units and if you can see them, and meeting the landlord directly. Otherwise you could end up with a very expensive mistake on your hands.

I drove up to an apartment complex in the neighbourhood of Parklands just outside the city, where a network of decent-looking developments had recently sprung up. The great thing about Parklands is that it is in walking and cycling distance from both the Central Business District and the entertainment district of Westlands. Parklands also has amenities that other middle-class or even upper-class neighbourhoods in Nairobi simply don't—pavements being just one key example. But also, as the heart of Nairobi's Indian community, the restaurants in Parklands serve more than boring knock-off European fare. Great schools, plentiful supermarkets, varied cuisine—really, for a middle-class Kenyan, Parklands is the dream.

There was just one problem. Building after building after building would not let me look at the apartments. I would knock, they would allow me to drive off the street and into the guest parking, but then the security guard wouldn't even let me out of the car before crowding me.

"I saw the 'to let' sign and I wanted to look at an apartment," I would say, with the car door half-open and only one foot on the ground.

"You can't," he would reply emphatically. "These are for the community."

"These are for the community". An emphatic euphemism for the racial segregation that still pervades many of the city's neighbourhoods. In Nairobi, there are residential blocks and neighbourhoods—tens, sometimes hundreds of apartments under unspoken but very real racial covenants that make it illegal for people of the wrong race to live in certain buildings or certain neighbourhoods. This is the capital's dirtiest and worst-kept secret. More than 100 years after the place of cool waters was settled, there are still parts of town where a person can be turned away from moving in because of their racial or sometimes ethnic identity. Nairobi's racial past still haunts the way residents organise their lives, and refusing to confront the reality of segregation impacts the extent to which the city can move forward in every regard.

The black-and-white dichotomy of race and racism has been the subject of much analysis and reflection across the world. The costs of racism at the extremes—where the perpetrator and the victim are at completely opposite ends of the spectrum of power, and so the injustice is very starkly clear—are more openly and thoroughly discussed, I think because the causes and consequences are so obvious. Less clear is what happens in the middle: the structural and physical racial violence that oppressed populations inflict on each other. How are we supposed to respond when the person projecting the racism is also a victim of the same system of oppression? What is the correct way to process this kind of racism, especially when the histories are complicated by violent antagonisms and reprisals that have never been apologised for?

Nairobi was built as a racially segregated town, and the legacy of racial cantonment has never been fully unpacked for various reasons. Crucially, many people in power benefit from the system of racial segregation, and so they have no interest in taking it apart. White communities draw the obvious benefits of sitting at the top of a hierarchy: doors open faster and presumptions of trustworthiness are given more freely. Asians can draw the benefits that come from proximity to whiteness. But the most powerful segments of the black population that inherited political power also benefit from a ready-made scapegoat when questions are asked about why the fruits of independence have not yet been equally distributed. Kenya is not the United States, where non-white communities are the minority—it's the opposite. The black majority is a tremendous one, both statistically and with significant control over the key aspects of society. But this also makes the situation a lot less linear than America's, in terms of assessing the problem and speaking it plainly and accurately so that it can be properly addressed.

This tension is painfully clear in the relationship between the Asian and black populations in Kenya, and the murky histories, fears and slights—real or perceived—that they inflict on each other. Statistically, Asians in Kenya amount to about 1 per cent of the national population, but they are an economically powerful and highly visible minority. In fact, Kenya has the continent's second largest population with roots in the Indian sub-continent after South Africa, despite dramatic declines in the size of that population since independence. Amongst a black-majority population, in a society where proximity to whiteness still confers tremendous, palpable advantages, where anti-black racism still pervades the popular discourse, but under a weighty history of oppression and violence from both the white and black faces of power, Kenyans of Asian descent occupy a curious and complicated space.

"This is for the community" is a representation of that complexity. Historically, Parklands was home to part of the city's Asian population—Indian families brought over as indentured and forced labourers to build the railway that connects Kampala to the sea, or traders and businessmen whose commercial acumen turned the city into an economic hub. Racial segregation is in the DNA of the city, where freedom of movement for the black population was violently controlled by the British pass systems, and residential neighbourhoods were strictly zoned by race. The only part of Nairobi with a measure of mixing was the Central Business District, where Asian business-owners ran shops and black men were allowed to work as clerks or lowly bureaucrats—always under the gaze of the racist settler state and with the threat of violent reprisal looming. Black families were forcefully separated under colonial rule because only black men were legally allowed to live and work in the city, and only for a certain number of years; by contrast, Asian families lived in designated neighbourhoods near the city, although they too were subject to the racist violence and vagaries of the colonial state.

The imprint of Nairobi's racist past still pervades the city. After independence, many white families left the city—or the country altogether—but many retreated to other towns in the agricultural and conservation-centred highlands, where they could build insular lives away from the majority-black population. Upwardly mobile black families, some of whom were well connected to power, moved into the empty houses and lots left behind, and so historically white neighbourhoods like Karen and Lavington had an influx of black families long before historically Asian areas like Parklands. Only after the economic collapse of the 1980s and 1990s, when many working-class Asian families left the country, did neighbourhoods like Ngara and Pangani see a massive influx of black residents. The single-family houses that had been built for the Asian population in the colonial period were eventually converted into densely populated apartment complexes of questionable architectural integrity, and formerly middle-class neighbourhoods quickly deteriorated into borderline slums.

Parklands stands as a hold-out against this trend. It's not that there aren't apartment blocks replacing single-family units there. But this neighbourhood was the last to switch from the single-family home model, and so it has the newest and most urbane developments. The owners of some of these complexes make it abundantly clear that they will not rent to outsiders. Sometimes this means they will not rent to non-Asians, sometimes it means they will not rent to people who are not of their own religious persuasion. Kenya hosts many of the main religious groups that are present in the Indian sub-continent—Hindus, Sikhs, Jains, Ismailis, Bohras, Ahmadi Muslims—but, considering that Kenyans of Asian descent account for only an estimated 1 per cent in a population of 47 million, some of these groups only have a few hundred members. For any group within this sub-group, to refuse to open up residential complexes to outsiders is quite a dramatic declaration of self-segregation, often against economic common sense.

So why would these communities pursue such an absurd choice? In part, because a significant portion of Kenya's South

Asian population is made up of recent arrivals who do not have the extensive knowledge of the country's fraught political history. Emigration of Kenya's Indians since independence has been dramatic, with many taking up British nationality, particularly during the most oppressive years of the one-party state. For the families that have stayed behind and resisted inter-marriage, the only option is to bring partners over from the sub-continent. Some large businesses also prefer to hire individuals from the sub-continent to manage their business concerns rather than hiring Africans. In 2019, for example, a large supermarket chain in Nairobi created a public storm when one of its marketing managers sent out a racist circular declaring that their most recent promotional campaign was targeting "European shoppers". When pushed, the supermarket's management admitted that the employee in question was not Kenyan.

And yet Kenya's constitution prohibits discrimination in all its forms, including housing discrimination. In the US, such informal policies were a cornerstone of the systemic discrimination practices put in place after the end of slavery to prevent free black people from moving into urban neighbourhoods. Renowned writer Lorraine Hansberry, author of the acclaimed play *A Raisin in the Sun*, was a victim of such discrimination; her own family's case against a neighbourhood association that was preventing sales to black families in Chicago is the precedent case that made such discrimination illegal. So, at least in other common-law jurisdictions, the court makes it clear that you cannot refuse to rent to a person because of their race or their religious affiliation. Why does this practice survive in modern Kenya, and so uncritically too?

Part of the challenge in having an open, honest conversation about race and racism in Kenya is that our history is filled with awkward silences and egregious violence between oppressed groups. This requires twice as much empathy to navigate as it would to think through racism between the white and black extremes. First of all, the word "Asian" itself carries a great deal of complexity, particularly with the recent arrival of a significant Chinese population that is continuing many of the same practices of self-segregation and separation. People from Asia in Kenya could also be descendants of the Omani community that settled and dominated the East African coast from the seventeenth century onwards. They could be connected to India's Hindu, Jain, or Sikh communities, or Pakistan's Bohras, Ismailis or Ahmadis. To the average Kenyan, all of these latter groups are "Indian", with all the baggage and complexity that comes with that mislabelling.

Kenya's Indian community was brought to the colony starting in 1895 as indentured labour—one step up from the forced labour of black people on the continent. These "coolies", as the British called them, were paid, but only on condition of their return to the sub-continent once the railway was completed. They were subject to the same caste-like system of racial segregation as the Kenyan-born population: separate public toilets, separate public fountains, separate rail carriages. The marginal advantage that the Indian community had was in the second-wave arrivals from the sub-continent and even from Southern Africa, who came over as businessmen, trained teachers and doctors, and were able to demand a touch more respect from the racist state. Indians under this structure paid more in taxes, were allowed to live in urban areas, and could run their own separate education and health systems.

It made sense that, when the African community began to agitate for independence, there were divisions within the Indian community. Some who were comfortable with the scraps from the colonial table didn't see a reason to join the liberation movement. Some representatives in the legislative council, for example—the main legislative body in the colony—thought that it was enough for the colonial state to provide marginally more opportunities to the black population, and to protect the advantages that Asians already had in the territory. They voted consistently with the white minority.

But some who felt that equality was a principle worth fighting for did join the struggle, representing Africans accused of treason in the kangaroo courts, providing shelter for fighters coming in from the countryside, and generally making themselves available for the fight for an independent Kenya. For instance, the Kenyan chapter of the Ghadar Party—an anti-imperialist movement of expatriate Indian origin, with branches all over the world—was established during the First World War. Many of its members were sentenced to death by the colonial administration for sedition and terrorism for simply belonging to the party. Makhan Singh, a revolutionary trade union leader, was imprisoned for eleven years by the British for using labour as an entry point in demanding equality for all races in the territory.

At independence, all Indians in the Kenya colony were given two years to take up Kenyan citizenship; but only 20,000 out of an estimated population of 180,000 did. Most chose British citizenship. The Kenyatta administration wasted no time in portraying this as an act of disloyalty. This about-face of the Kenyatta government after independence—from comrade to accuser—must have come as a complete surprise to many of those who stood by the African population. Tellingly, the first high-profile assassination in independent Kenya was of Pio Gama Pinto, a Kenyan of Goan descent who had not only founded the official newspaper of the liberation party, but also worked as a lawyer defending many of Africa's high-profile independence leaders. The facts of this 1965 assassination have never been resolved, but some have pointed to the increasingly fraught ideological politics of the time. Pinto was an avowed communist; Kenyatta was a committed mercenary capitalist with strong ties to countries like the US and even the UK. In any case, Pinto's assassination must have fed into the increasing exodus of Asians from Kenya. The population dwindled, and those who remained began a slow withdrawal from public life.

Between the 1970s and 1980s, Kenya's Indian community was a target for a great deal of extortion and intimidation from the one-party state, in part because of its relative prosperity. All the marginal advantages of colonisation had been an enormous head-start for Kenya's white and Asian populations; but, unlike the white families who had largely retreated to the countryside, Kenya's Asians remained visible in the cities. The unspoken consensus was that you could stay in Kenya and participate in whatever business you wanted to—as long as you didn't try to get involved in politics. The one-party state worked hard to emphasise that those in the country of Indian heritage were outsiders and not "real Kenyans", who "did not participate fully" in activities required of citizens to show loyalty to the state. In 1979 a district commissioner in Kakamega threatened severe action against Indians who had stayed away from Kenyatta Day celebrations. In 1980 an assistant minister—incidentally, a white Kenyan—accused Kenya's Indians of not participating in national charitable initiatives. This all came to a head in 1982, when then President Moi accused Indian business of sabotage for having invested money abroad.

The August 1982 attempted coup was an inflection point in Kenyan politics, including the relationship between the country's various groups. It gave rise to the darkest era of authoritarianism in the independent nation and to unchecked violence and discrimination against many groups. Many of the stories of the coup have never been fully told, particularly as the state repression mechanism—including censorship of the media—went into full gear, and many victims of the violence during that period elected to withdraw from society rather than speak publicly of their experiences. News reports confirm that Indian shops were vandalised and several Indian women were raped—some attest that they were raped by security forces rather than the coup leaders. The slow exodus that had started with the Pinto assassination seventeen years before now accelerated dramatically over the next decade.

At the same time, hostility from the Indian community against the African population rose. Newspaper reports from the 1980s have a number of articles decrying this racism against the black majority. For example, even in 1983, *The Standard* published an article with examples of businesses that refused to rent to Africans. Some of the pieces claiming to decry the racism were racist themselves, for instance a 1983 op-ed from the official mouthpiece of the ruling party, *The Kenya Times*, which calls Kenya's Indians "rich, miserly, secretive, arrogant, contemptuous against Africans and insular". The insularity charge is difficult to rebut—in 1979 British-Indian writer V.S. Naipaul visited Kenya and noted that "the Indian in East Africa has brought India with him and kept it inviolate".

This is the complex history in which today's racial relationship between Indians (in the broader, Kenyan sense of the word) and Africans must be explored. It is also a context in which white supremacy is still very much an issue, and proximity to whiteness does confer clear privileges. It is a context in which both sides have credible histories of mutual aid and mutual harm. It is a Kenya in which Zarina Patel and Wangarī Maathai fight to protect public spaces for all Kenyans, but members of their extended communities still won't rent spaces to each other or allow their children to attend each other's schools. It is a case where there is plenty of blame to go around, but the calculus for determining how much blame gets apportioned to whom and for what is difficult to nail down.

It is also a situation in which a number of Asians—including Chinese arrivals—are recent transplants who do not have the collective memory of these connections and disconnections between the black and brown populations. The histories of Pio Gama Pinto, Makhan Singh and Zarina Patel are very poorly taught in Kenya's education system, and not taught at all in the British-curriculum schools that many Kenyan Indians attend. In this ignorance, empathy and open-mindedness wilt and the two communities learn to see each other through overly simplified lenses that heighten disconnection and emphasise difference. But even for those who do remember, there is so little room to remember together, as each community retreats to their racial cocoons after the working day is done—separate schools, separate restaurants, separate shopping centres, separate social spaces—circulating within their bubbles and never really living in the same city.

This means that many reactions to events in modern times are loaded with collective memories shrouded in silence and unspoken fears, historical angers and vengefulness that are difficult to work against because the initial slights underlying them have never been acknowledged or discussed. We are raised to be angry about things that our grandparents are too traumatised to speak about openly. We use racist language to criticise racist acts, becoming the thing we claim to oppose because we need the sharpness of our tongues to compensate for the muted responses from power. We fight each other more violently and more aggressively for the small advantages we have over each other, rather than for a just and equal world.

I interpret "This is for the community" as an attempt to carve out a space of safety from a poorly constructed and ill-perceived threat. In a country where elections routinely lead to ethnic violence, and where racial violence has never truly been addressed, my perhaps-too-generous interpretation is that this is about trying to protect the ethnie. That rationale doesn't make it right. It only makes it more urgent to work against the fractures that divide society. It is still very much illegal and immoral for a building to exclude people on the basis of race.

There's no walking back from the racism that black Africans have endured at the hands of Asians in their own country. There's equally no walking back from the fact that Kenyan Indians have been the targets for unjust state violence and criminal violence because of their race. Being Asian in Kenya has created specific vulnerabilities that cannot be erased simply through proximity to whiteness, but being black in a society where proximity to whiteness confers advantages creates specific aggressions that members of the Indian community have inflicted on the black community.

Race is a construction built on malleable hierarchies that serve specific political functions, but the benefits for those lower in the hierarchies are extremely slim. More often than not, the divisions between those lower down the totem pole are crucial in helping the most powerful groups retain their dominance. Playing up the differences between Indians and Africans was a cornerstone of British colonial policy, perhaps quite simply because the white settlers were outnumbered by those they claimed to dominate. Indians at the time were more educated and more organised than Africans, who were enduring their first experiences of colonisation—offering them enough scraps to keep them sated and distracted from the work of collective freedom was a way of preventing them from providing the tactical support that black Kenyans needed to push for their independence.

It is quite something that the best-known figure of Indian independence—Mahatma Gandhi—saw himself during his time in apartheid South Africa as having more in common with the white population than with the "kaffirs". One of Gandhi's biographers, the former *New York Times* editor Joseph Lelyveld, says in unambiguous terms that "he was a racist", agreeing that white supremacy in South Africa was natural, and that black people are "troublesome, very dirty and live like animals". This was the same Gandhi who would return to India to successfully agitate for independence from white rule. This speaks to how insidious and toxic proximity to whiteness can be as a doctrine for divide and rule, and why it was a tried and tested tactic in the settler colonies of South Africa, Zimbabwe, Zambia, Botswana, Namibia, Senegal, Algeria and others. By disentangling the liberation of one group from the other, the coloniser had fewer groups to fight.

In 2017 the Kenyan government officially recognised Indians as the forty-fourth "tribe". This acknowledgement comes around every few decades, when the ruling class decides not to unravel the ethnic politics of the country but to bring more groups into the mix in order to increase opportunities for profiteering in the political space. The announcement was received with lukewarm enthusiasm—the label "Indian", used in that way, denies the diversity of the South Asian community in Kenya, and is employed to cover a complex, multi-faceted experience. Especially coming in an election year, the intent behind the 2017 declaration was quickly discerned—"Indians" were to be another pawn in the never-ending ethnic games that the powerful play in Kenya.

But, in the same year, a group of three women called The LAM Sisterhood—two black and one of South Asian descent—put on a play celebrating strong women throughout Kenyan history. There was Field Marshal Muthoni, who joined the Freedom and Land Army (Mau Mau) when she was sixteen to fight for Kenya's independence. After independence there was Zarina Patel, who took on the authoritarian Moi regime to defend the last green space in Nairobi's Central Business District. There was Professor Wangarī Maathai, who fought the same fight for other green spaces in the city and became the first African woman to win the Nobel Peace Prize. I saw the play, and I think it did something more important for the relationship between Kenya's black and Asian populations than any state-driven declaration. It created a space to celebrate the things that bring society together, while turning a critical eye on how power divides—proving once again that feminism can do more to heal the wounds of a fragmented post-colonial state than patriarchal notions of power that only seek to replace one type of strongman with another.

"This is for the community" needs spaces like this, which allow for fraught conversations that recognise the violent histories between Kenya's communities. "This is for the community" could be reclaimed to mean something new, healing and necessary. Movement and mobility between societies triggers a demand for reciprocity—if Kenyans hope for the world to open its doors, then we'll have to figure out how to open the doors we've closed on each other.

12

SMALL ACTS OF RESISTANCE

The first time I went to the Democratic Republic of Congo, I didn't fly directly from Nairobi. I was going to Kinshasa, so the cheapest option was to fly via Addis Ababa. This was the trip that impressed upon me just how large the DRC—and by extension Africa—is. Straddling the Equator with a toe in the Atlantic Ocean, the DRC has the most international borders of any country on the continent: nine neighbours and tens of border crossings, official and unofficial. The DRC is in effect four countries—the Lingala, Kikongo, Kiswahili and Tshiluba regions, and the estimated 600 languages within them, bound together by the absurdities of colonisation. It takes five hours to fly across the country at its widest point, and even its second and third largest cities are bigger than the capitals of most other African states. I have never before nor ever again been so completely intimidated by an African country, nor so fascinated by how much it captures the best and the worst of what people can do to each other.

The contemporary history of the DRC is always discussed as a litany of what could have been. What could the country have been without Leopold II's poisonous colonial rule? What could the country have been if Lumumba had not been assassinated? Where would the most resource-rich country in Africa have been without the murderous regime of Mobutu Sese Seko? Would the war in the East be going differently if Laurent Kabila had never been handpicked as the face of the movement to overthrow him? Because the brief glimpses of stability and prosperity in the DRC are so brilliant: the first nuclear energy plant in Africa, which now lies rotting and defunct; Lumumba's young sparkling mind, so clearly articulating the challenges of the post-colony; the country finding itself the global source for the most in-demand mineral of the digital age—we always measure what is against what could have been. The D in DRC may well stand for desideria, as every victory and loss is tinged with nostalgia for a past that never was.

I think about the DRC a lot when I look at my phone. It reminds me of both my time there and the general story of the country. The first time I visited, I was doing humanitarian work as an intern in both Kinshasa and Kindu, the small regional capital of the province of Maniema. The next few times, I crossed the border from Rwanda and visited Goma, the largest city in the East, to meet with human rights defenders working in the town and to conduct training on how to use mobile phones to record human rights abuses. The few times after that, I crossed the border again into Bukavu, to work with lawyers and human rights defenders on using video evidence to build cases against violators. Each of those experiences spun around using my phone to document, to teach and to push back against the criminal enterprises that had turned fracture lines in the community into an opportunity for profit. Part of the work involved watching videos of human rights atrocities, in order to teach people how to properly document them and build advocacy around them. It was a difficult job, but nothing compared to the people who lived with that reality long after I had left. I was there, ostensibly, to do a small, small part, helping people who were trying to end the war to do so safely. But the more I learnt about the DRC, the more I realised that the thing in my hand was part of the problem I claimed I was trying to solve.

The contemporary tragedy of the DRC is inseparable from the tragedy of the mobile phone. The DRC is the world's largest exporter of coltan, a core ingredient of the parts that make electronics possible. Research has connected the hunger for coltan to the conflict in the Eastern Congo, which is one of the world's most devastating wars, seemingly with no end in sight. Armed groups control territories with coltan stocks and profit directly from selling them on the global market. Some groups also steal coltan from legal sources—hijacking shipments, or putting up violent roadblocks where they impose unofficial taxes on shipments. Working conditions in the mines can also be appalling. Children are exploited as miners, and whole communities are taken hostage in order to keep the mines running. Unlike blood diamonds that have had the Hollywood treatment, leading to heightened scrutiny and changes in attitudes, coltan is yet to gain much public awareness. Most people don't even know what coltan is. But I do.

What are you supposed to do when you know something bad is happening somewhere else in the world and one of the things that you depend on for your life and existence is part of the problem? We know that plastic is bad. We know that soft drinks and beers exacerbate water injustice, particularly in poor countries. We know by now that most of our clothes are made by people who get paid a pittance and in exploitative conditions. The question is, what do we as individual consumers do about it? Are we ready to give up plastic, soft drinks and cheap fashion altogether? Does knowing that the decision has life-or-death consequences for people make that choice simpler?

I wish I could write that my time in the DRC has left me more categorical about these things. I can say that perhaps I see a lot less grey than most people do, because I have seen the videos of women sexually assaulted by guards at coltan mines making sure that they are not smuggling grams of the precious substance out of their vaginas or anuses. Experiencing the DRC as a real place gave these concerns form and purpose, and while I can't say that I have completely given up electronics, I am certainly more cautious about how I use what I do have, to make sure that I get bang for my buck. I've learnt the value of individual choice in the grand milieu of making a difference, by showing up to witness the excess of conflict in this complicated country. I still use my phone; I just feel incredibly guilty about it, and I find myself constantly thinking about ways of reducing my footprint on this political economy.

I've settled on a model of individual activism that tries to make each daily decision as categorical as I can. It can be tempting to think that activism and advocacy are big and complex things that can only be achieved by powerful people, but the older I get the more I'm convinced of the power of small acts of resistance, even if—or especially if—no one else knows that we are doing them. You don't have to take out a billboard and beat all of your friends over the head with your choices; you just have to make them.

I have a very ambivalent relationship with mobile phones. Because I move around so much, I love being able to talk to best friends scattered all over the world. If I could, I would still be using my old Blackberry for communications, but I do enjoy the camera function on the phone I currently have. And, like I said, I have watched people use phones to demand social justice in contexts where those demands would otherwise just be impossible. I have seen people build movements for social change within their societies—create a platform and get heard even when the rest of the world would rather not listen—simply by being strategic about how they use their phones.

But mobile phones are perhaps the best example of the damage done by a global economy built entirely on endless consumption for the people who make the things that we consume. A mobile phone is designed to go out of fashion and out of function within a very short window of time—sometimes within a year for the more expensive models. That phone that you love goes from carrying a full charge for twelve to fifteen hours to needing a full charge every three or four, because within a year you're supposed to lust after the next new model. The tragedy of building things that are designed to turn into waste is not just limited to the person who enjoys using them. It is also a tragedy for our lands and oceans, because we haven't fully figured out what to do with our electronic waste—except ship it out to landfills in poor countries where they poison the water and the people around it.

People still wait in line to replace their phones with the newest model even when the "old" one still works perfectly—even those same people who say that they would never buy a conflict diamond. Those who should know better aren't going far enough to connect our personal choices to the way the world works, and so it is difficult to imagine what accountability for causing this harm would look like. Integrated supply chains for goods like coltan, which start in the developing world and end in the developed world, necessarily involve people in every socio-economic class. The opportunities for exploitation are everywhere, especially as large corporations that only focus on profitability or growth resort to more desperate measures in order to protect their advantage. Why pay more for conflict-free coltan when you can get it cheaply and relatively reliably from an unstable and dangerous DRC? Why encourage your consumers to curb unnecessary consumption when that unnecessary consumption is what keeps your industry afloat?

The absurd ends of this situation are everywhere. People need mobile phones to communicate, but because the company must not only grow, but keep growing indefinitely, companies introduce all kinds of strange bottlenecks and obstacles to force customers to pay extra for services. They not only charge exorbitant rates, but encourage their customers to ignore all the suffering that their products cause. The networks that dominate markets in countries like the US are often able to do this by giving customers a choice: between being locked into long and expensive contracts, or accepting sub-par service on pre-paid phones. They offer you benefits you don't want but can't decline, and charge you extra for the things that you need but can't get as a default (like receiving calls). The difference in quality between pre-paid and contract phones is palpable—it's the difference between being able to receive a call while indoors and having to stand outside in the snow looking for signal. Companies create and maintain these two levels of service because they can get away with it—it costs more to get out of your contract than it does to get a new pre-paid phone. The messaging is clear: to get any kind of meaningful service, get the most expensive phone your budget can handle.

In the US, the contract system has fuelled an endless cycle of demand and planned obsolescence that left me angry and frustrated after my first trips to the DRC. The company has no incentive to make it easier for you to repair or replace your existing phone with a used one, nor does it make sense for you to pay substantial amounts of money for sub-par service. Forget about that insurance you have been loyally paying every month for eventualities exactly such as these. Given the way the insurance industry is set up, the co-pay—money that you need to hand over in order to claim the benefits of your policy—is more expensive than what you would pay to take a step down and accept the sub-par pay-as-you-go phone. There is deliberately no incentive to be more careful with your phone or to repair it when it breaks down.

Consumers should be able to opt out of this set-up, but it's difficult to see how. Even the companies that claim to be producing ethical products face the challenge of proving those claims. I once bought a phone that claimed to be fully conflict-free, accepting that an inferior camera was just part of the package in trying to do the right thing. But a little digging revealed that the market for coltan is deliberately designed to obstruct tracing— the process of identifying exactly where your coltan came from. It is difficult for any company to genuinely claim that their coltan is 100 per cent conflict-free because all the mixing happens at the middlemen level. Unless you escort the coltan shipment all the way from the ground to the factory where it is processed into circuit boards, you can't, with the current state of the system, prove it with absolute certainty.

Moving between the DRC and the US, and having to exist within this ethical nightmare, was challenging to say the least. Can you pretend to un-see the systemic violence that a market structure inflicts on the other side of the world if you have witnessed its consequences first-hand? Or if you decide to pretend not to notice, what other aspects of your hard-won moral education will you then rationalise away, just to be able to navigate your new reality? If I gave up and gave in to this structure, having seen those videos and listened to those testimonies, what else would I be prepared to give up for my own comfort, even at the expense of other people's survival?

This tension compelled me to think more completely about my own little power and agency. Wangarī Maathai, the first African woman to win the Nobel Peace Prize, spoke extensively about the importance of individual agency in environmental protection. She herself was violently beaten, castigated and tormented for taking a stand for the environment under Kenya's authoritarian rule, at a time when women were discouraged from having a public presence at all, let alone using it for activism against the state. Individual actions matter, even if they only matter to the person who is doing them—even if they only make it easier for us to square the circle of living the lives we live.

It's not easy to opt for conscious consumption in a country where excess consumption is celebrated as a human right and as a civic duty. Where the choice is so considerably constrained by manufacturers, it would be easier and more comfortable to close one's eyes and just go along with it. But there is always space for everyday activism, and the cumulative impact of this individual agency can have consequences bigger than we imagine. The diamond industry was once even more of a systematic monopoly than the mobile phone industry in the US today, but even De Beers has had to yield a little bit to pressure to address human rights concerns over conflict diamonds. Imagine what would happen if not even all but many mobile phone consumers in the US and around the world communicated to their providers that they were unwilling to be part of a market that profited from the suffering of others, while treating its customers with such flagrant disregard? Imagine if we pushed the people who make our phones to stop creating conditions for endless and ultimately meaningless consumption? If we told them we would rather repair the old phones we had instead of constantly being pressured to replace them?

I like nice things as much as the next person so I can't in good conscience say that I've found a perfect way of reconciling all of these contradictions. What I've found is space within my decision-making matrix for small acts of resistance that make it easier for me to sleep at night. What I have done is achieve a space where, when I look at my phone, I don't only feel guilt. The mobile phone conversation is just one example of how these tensions play out in the real world—how abstract conversations about morality and consumption look at the concrete level of choice. But I think it's increasingly important for more of us to lean into the discomfort of these questions, so that we can give ourselves or the generations that come after us a fighting chance at resolving them.

13

WHO DO YOU SAY I AM?

When I was 18 years old, I went along with my classmates to the local chief's office to apply for my national identity card. As in most Kenyan high schools, every year, the members of the final class (Form Four) were taken to the nearest chief's camp and guided by a supervising teacher through this rite of passage. Technically, the process of applying for the card is supposed to be straightforward—the ID card is theoretically a right, because it allows you access to all government buildings, to a bank account, and to cross regional borders without a passport. In many ways, it allows the Kenyan adult to access the privileges of citizenship. It should be an entitlement. Sadly for me and millions of other Kenyans across the country, the process of applying for an identity card was far from straightforward, and this would be my first and most personal lesson in the politics of citizenship in the contemporary Kenyan state.

If you think about it, the idea that an individual's personhood can be rooted to one place and then distilled to information fitting on a 2-by-1-inch laminated card is absurd. We are born outside marriage or in unrecognised marriages; we move, we marry, we divorce, we meet people who make us love one place more than the place we have spent most of our lives; our parents die, or they split up and we choose to live with one and not the other. Yet there are more countries requiring identity cards than not. All of which would be unproblematic, if states didn't restrict access to them to specific groups, only to persecute people on the other end for not having them.

In 2015, hundreds of Somalis—numbers remain murky given restricted access—many of whom had full Kenyan citizenship, were detained in the country's largest stadium, and it was because the government said they did not have identity cards. Nubian Kenyans—descendants of South Sudanese soldiers brought over to fight for the British during the independence war—cannot get identity documents, and therefore struggle to exist as full adult citizens in Kenya, including registering their births and deaths. Kenya is littered with conditional citizens, and if there is a physical document that illustrates how pervasive and dangerous this is, it is the ID card.

An ID card shouldn't make a person. Why should the administrative state have the power to decide who does or does not exist? This is exactly what the politics of the ID card in Kenya has become. There is no state–citizen relationship, only a state–subject relationship in which the state exerts near-absolute power over the individual and their ability to occupy space within the territory, and can even withhold from them the benefits of fully existing.

The identity card in Kenya is a direct descendant of the colonial-era pass that Africans in urban areas were required to have on their person at all times, particularly where they were likely to encounter Europeans. During this time, it was a metal plate—a large dog tag—that identified the person, his father, his grandfather, his place of birth and his employer, so that the person "responsible" for the African could be easily contacted if the African was found to be out of place. Out of place, because all major cities in Kenya were racially segregated, and the pass was a method of keeping Africans out of European and Asian areas especially. My grandfather, based in Nairobi while he worked with the East African Railway Corporation, was forced to wear a pass, and on the singular occasion that I asked him about it, I recall seeing him visibly recoil with something that looked a lot like shame. It was a mark of dehumanisation. The pass took something from him: the young man who moved freely in pursuit of the things that young men chase after was gone, and instead he was tied to a place and to a person that he barely knew.

The pass was about excluding and including. You literally took on the shame of being branded and tagged like an animal for the apparent freedom to join a group of Africans allowed to move relatively freely within a place. You were subjected to the daily shame of wearing your inferiority around your neck, in exchange for the relative security of not being harassed, not being rounded up like a pack of stray dogs, not being huddled into a prison cell and humiliated by guards for their entertainment. The pass was protection against "deportation" to the "reserves"—overcrowded rural spaces where many Africans had been moved to free up fertile land for colonial plantations.

Kenyan adults aren't today required to wear metal plates around their necks, but they are required to carry around a small card, without which they can't enter or exit buildings, get married, register their children or do a whole laundry list of other things. That speaks volumes as to the state's failure to exorcise the demons of colonialism and its inherited desire to create categories and assign benefits of belonging. Of my entire high school class, two of us were told that we could not get identity cards that day. One was my colleague, a Kenyan Somali, who—although he had been born and raised in the

South C neighbourhood of Nairobi—was told he had to return to his grandfather's hometown of Mandera, almost six hours away, and apply for his identity card there: "You couldn't possibly be from Nairobi."

I was denied an ID card on the same premise. I'm not Somali, but even though my family had lived in Nairobi for almost sixty years, this inheritance was on my mother's side, and Kenyans are required to use their father's identity documents to prove citizenship. Never mind that my father died long before I applied for the card. The chief issuing the ID cards expected me to make the full day's journey across the country to return to a village I had never lived in, and ask a man I had never met to affirm my identity through my father's lineage, down to the smallest administrative unit. The suggestion is that children cannot live except through their fathers, nor outside the categories created by the state. These are not small hurdles—they are major acts of discrimination targeting people based on their ethnic identities and nothing else. People from certain groups receive their ID cards in the city automatically; the rest of us are constantly reminded that we don't fully belong. For the millions of Kenyans who endure this type of administrative harassment, it's yet another reminder that some people are more Kenyan than others.

A country with a critical mass of contingent citizens is hardly a country at all. The fault line fracturing Kenya's politics hinges on ethnicity precisely because the government has woven together all of these high-stakes issues of belonging and identity, and imposed them on something that is highly fluid and malleable. We keep falling apart along these lines because they are so transient, yet somehow the basis for everything. Kenya's incomplete separation from the ID card system and its social consequences is part of a broader problem of knitting the country together, and fixing the problems of the system—removing the contingencies on citizenship is part of healing what hurts.

I had the luxury of opting out. I could define myself differently because I already had a passport and a driver's licence. But for millions of Kenyans, travelling abroad or driving a car is not an option. Applying for an identity card means reckoning with a state that has a constantly narrowing definition of who you cannot be. It is the humiliation of being told you could not possibly belong to the only place you have ever called home. It is being asked to look up that father who left you, or that village that forced you to leave. It is rejection. More importantly, for the people facing arbitrary arrest and detention—as they did in 2013 after the Westgate attack—it is the ever-present risk of extortion and violence from your own government. It is the exchange of ever-increasing sums of money for a tenuous recognition of your fundamental right to be protected; protected not least from being arbitrarily stripped of the benefits of citizenship.

But today ID cards are all the rage in countries around the world. India has launched the much denigrated Aadhaar system, a "single source of truth" ID programme that not only identifies the person before the state but which, in its absence, leads to millions of people being denied access to benefits from the state. The system is connected to the national population registry, and with that the idea of "rightful" citizens. But who gets to be a rightful citizen is defined by the state and its ethno-nationalisms, and as religious fundamentalism has permeated the highest levels of Indian governance, that definition increasingly reflects the interests and privileges of power. In Assam state, millions of Muslim people are facing indefinite detention and expulsion on suspicion of being "foreign"—coming from Bangladesh or Myanmar.

Yet there are several reasons why a full citizen of Assam would not have acquired the card. They may not have had any contact with the government up to that point—the lived reality of millions of people in rural areas around the world. Some people have no fingerprints because of the nature of the work that they do, farmers and miners especially—yet biometrics are a cornerstone of the identity regime. Some people might have received their citizenship from a female parent in a patriarchal system.

More importantly, counting people better doesn't logically lead to better service provision, if the services were not being provided in the first place. Excluding millions of people wholesale because of their identity isn't going to make governments more interested in having their hospitals run better. Ultimately, it backs up the illusion of scarcity: that there aren't enough public goods available for everyone within the territory to receive them. There are other ways of determining identity that do not depend on un-humaning the person in this way. You could, for example—and this is a radical proposition—ask them. Or their neighbours.

In the *Hansard*—the record of British parliamentary debates going all the way back to 1915—the logic and argument behind Kenya keeping the ID system is tricky to discern. The debates are illuminating, not least because you see starkly the negotiated nature of Kenya's independence. Where African countries before independence were militant and categorical, after independence their opposition to the colonial state's tools of oppression become qualified and mealy-mouthed. The break between colonisation and independence was not complete, and a lot of the tools that had been explicitly designed to control the African population did not go away. We kept the prisons. We kept the colonial police. We kept the ID cards.

These cards and the systems built around them are a reminder that not only does the state have a monopoly on the use of force against you, but it also has the capacity to define who you are, independent of your participation. A Nairobi resident with documents that prove their residency—bank statements, passports, driver's licences and the like—can still be defined as a rural resident by a chief at the sub-location. A person born into a family with parents of different ethnic identities can be forced to choose their father's. The ID is not about who you are, but who the state says you are. You are reminded constantly and subtly, based on who can get that magical card and who cannot, that your citizenship is contingent, and can be withdrawn at will.

As a teenager, I didn't think too much of what it meant that an independent African state insisted on carrying on the degrading tradition of tagging citizens like cattle, a modernised but still problematic echo of the tactics that had been used to humiliate my grandfather. What I struggled with—albeit less eloquently then—were the gendered notions of self that the ID card perpetuated: this idea that I could only inherit identity from my father. I was frustrated by the idea that the state wanted to bind me more to an ethnic identity I had not yet embraced; to a place I had barely seen. I opted out, and embraced my national identity instead. I eventually got my ID card, because I could afford to wait it out, but I have trouble with the idea that in independent Kenya, almost fifty years after independence, I have still endured the same humiliations that my grandfather did.

14

SAGARMATHA

During the three weeks I was in Nepal in 2019, my guide constantly refused to refill my water. It began almost on the first day. He had asked that everyone buy a Nalgene water bottle, but I didn't want to buy one because I preferred to carry a water pack on my back. That was how I had summited both Mount Kenya (4,948 metres) and Mount Kilimanjaro (5,898 metres). We got into a back and forth at one of the rest houses and he refused to speak to me directly for the rest of the trip. But he also refused to refill my water bottle, and I didn't want to keep buying plastic ones, because that garbage all remains on the mountain after you've gone home.

It was not lost on me that I was the only black woman in my group. It wasn't lost on the rest of the group that he spoke to me in a way he absolutely did not speak to other people. By the time I got sick, he had already picked his favourites, and I was certainly not one of them. But I didn't care, because I was not on that mountain to make friends. I was on the mountain to get away from the pressures of an exhausting work schedule and, in fact, I really was happier with people leaving me alone.

But I needed water. Because hiking for eleven to twelve hours a day is an intense experience. The Himalayas are high and cold, so most days you are sweating profusely and you don't see it. If you don't moderate your water intake, it is very easy to grow dehydrated; and where dehydration happens, altitude sickness isn't far behind. A couple of days in, I got sick of waiting for them to provide me with water; so I bought a 1-litre plastic bottle and nursed it over dinner. And then I got angry. Truly and viscerally angry that I had been saving for this trip for months and was being treated this shabbily. I hated that I was almost fully dependent on people who did not have my best interests at heart. I went to bed angry.

From around the third day of the trip, in order to get my water pack refilled, I had to ask a white Australian man in the group to ask the guide on my behalf. Otherwise, I would not have had water. One night, the Australian guy showed up late, and so I was freezing and overtaxed; I still had not had any water by the time I went to bed. In the small hours of that morning, there was a moment when my mind began to slowly shut down, because I couldn't get my lungs to work.

It's the kind of thing that you go through alone, and it reminds you that we are all in this world alone—because no one will really understand how different you are from the person you were before. I am grateful to be alive, truly. But I also recognise that I am fundamentally changed. Sometimes the events of those forty-eight hours replay themselves in my mind involuntarily and my heart starts racing and I get scared all over again, because I remember that I nearly died. Not in a hypothetical or abstract way, but in a very immediate sense.

My mother still doesn't know this story.

The day before, we had done a practice hike up and down a small hill by the camp in Dingboche (4,300 metres), to test our altitude. I couldn't finish the hike. I'd gone a few metres up the mountain and sat down. The air was too thin. My legs were tired. I was dehydrated. And I was still angry. My heart just wasn't in it any more. I wanted to see the sun and I wanted to go home. But how can you go home fourteen days into a twenty-one-day hike? So I'd done what everyone says you should do—I'd tried to push through.

The next day, we made the push for Lobuche (4,900 metres). I don't think I have ever struggled quite so hard to gain 500 metres of altitude. I was just really fucking pissed. But also, I was getting sick, and my body knew it before my mind did. Because I was moving so slowly, the weather turned while I was still outside, and I got snowed on for almost an hour. I was getting weaker and weaker by the hour. I was also getting little, frigid snowflakes down the back of my jacket; not only was I cold, but I wasn't generating enough heat to get warmer.

I finally arrived in Lobuche in the afternoon—about two hours before everyone else in the group. As usual, the tea hut was overcrowded and the heat was far from optimal. I was freezing and shivering and—this is important—I couldn't get the shivering to stop. I sat by the fire for a few minutes but I couldn't get warm. To put it figuratively, the cold was in my bones. But not so figurative—my ribs actually started to hurt from the shivering. My teeth were chattering. And so I decided to go to bed and try and get warm, under my sleeping bag, another sleeping bag, two blankets and a hot water bottle.

The first sign that something wasn't right was that I couldn't stop getting up to pee. Every thirty to forty minutes, I would have to go to the bathroom. I had already lost a lot of water, I think, and here I was losing more. I tried to replace each pee with a chug on a bottle of water with electrolytes in it, but it would just run through me. Drink, pee. Drink, pee. Drink, pee. I hadn't had dinner, but I knew that if I had, that would not have ended well either. All the way until around one in the morning.

That was when I got this feeling in my chest. You know when you get acidity because you've eaten too fast or you've eaten something that doesn't agree with you? Every time I lay on my stomach, I would get this pain under my ribs like that same discomfort. The problem was, I needed to lie on my stomach to get warm, so that I could sleep. But every time I tried, there was that pain again. So I got up, and asked for the guide.

This wasn't the leader of our group who had refused to refill my water, but an assistant in training. He came in and offered me an antacid, and sat with me for a few minutes while I explained all the things that were happening. I still couldn't quite put my finger on it but I felt like all was not well in my body. I tried to go back to sleep.

By two in the morning, I still had not slept, but now I was having trouble breathing. I would inhale deeply and count to seven before exhaling at a slow count, but it was like I just couldn't get enough air in my lungs. Plus I was getting anxious, because the next morning we were scheduled to depart at 6 a.m. I wanted to sleep at least a little that night. But nothing was happening. Every time I tried to close my eyes and drop the counting, I would get short of breath and have to get up again. So I asked for the guide, again.

I told him that I was having trouble breathing and he sat with me for a few minutes. By this point, I was inhaling deeply and audibly. I kept trying to roll my neck and relax my shoulders, sitting up straight so that more air would enter my lungs. But it wasn't going so well. I just wasn't getting enough air. So I asked for an oxygen tank. I just needed to breathe properly for a few minutes so I could sleep.

The main guide brought in the oxygen tank, but there was a problem. None of them could figure out how it worked. Keep in mind that I hadn't shorted myself on this trip. I'm the kind of person who takes risks, but I try to only take calculated risks. I'm not going to do a bungee jump or a sky dive with a bargain company just to save a couple of dollars. If I want to do something risky, I try to mitigate that risk by going with the best. This was not a cheap company—it was highly recommended by people I knew and by people who had trekked the Himalayas before. This was the easiest of the hikes they had on offer, from Lukla to Everest Base Camp. But here I was at 3 a.m., struggling to breathe and watching two men struggling to figure out the oxygen tank.

I don't think it helped my anxiety much. It made it worse, and the more anxious I got the worse my breathing got. I watched them panicking and flailing around in Nepalese or Sherpa while I tried to slow-count my breaths into some kind of steady rhythm. The first hour went by. Then the second. Suddenly, it was 4 a.m., and I hadn't had a proper breath of air for almost three hours. I started to get dizzy and feel a little faint. Now I absolutely couldn't breathe.

There wasn't a moment when everything started to collapse. It wasn't that something specifically happened. My body just started getting tired. Suddenly, the only thing I wanted, more than anything else in the world, was to close my eyes and just rest. I felt like I had been fighting for air for so long and I just wanted to stop fighting. I couldn't tell you what part of my brain realised this was a bad idea, but instinctively I just knew. Don't fall asleep, Nanjala. Don't fall asleep.

So I started reciting my travel information out loud. I then moved to reciting the alphabet backwards, like I had been pulled over because they thought I was drink-driving. And I don't know when this happened, but they told me later that at some point the things I was saying stopped making any sense. That my lips were moving, but what was coming out of my mouth wasn't what I thought it was.

Thankfully, one of the members of my group was a nurse. At 5 a.m. the two young men finally decided to ask for help, and she helped them figure out how to run the oxygen tank. They strapped it over my face and after a few deep breaths I fell asleep almost immediately. But first, I texted my friend in Washington DC:

"Are you awake?"

"Yes"

"I need to tell you something but I need you not to freak out."

"Okay"

"I'm in Nepal and I'm having trouble breathing. I need you to text my insurance company and get me out of here. Here's a copy of my insurance certificate with all the contact details. Please hurry."

I still haven't told my mother this story because when I'd come back from Kilimanjaro I had stubbed both my big toes and had massive blood clots underneath my nails that had turned them blue. It took nine months for those clots to clear and for the nails to grow out. By travelling the world the way I do—jumping out of planes and off bridges, climbing high mountains and picking random places on a map just to go and watch the sunrise—I am already living a life that she struggles to understand. Adding the dangers and risks underneath to the mix would just make things more complicated. Over three years after Kilimanjaro, I still got lectures about what that relatively gentle hike did to my toes. But I wouldn't change my Kilimanjaro experience for the world. It was difficult, but I'd never once felt like I was pulling against my guides for reasons that I couldn't do anything about.

A lot of the challenges that I faced in Nepal had to do with the conveyor belt that is Mount Everest. I think that the seduction of even coming close to climbing the highest mountain in the world attracts a certain type of person. I know this person because I am this person. Insanely driven. Single-minded. Achievement-oriented. But there are things that can be done to help such people manage the challenge of mountain-climbing, and on Sagarmatha, all of those things are falling away. The mountain is Nepal's biggest foreign-exchange-earner, so there is far less scrutiny of the companies offering climbs or of the people taking them. The routes are crowded, so when I fell ill, instead of being able to stay a day longer to recover, I was given a stark choice—keep moving or evacuate, but you can't stay here because someone else is coming for this bed. My Kilimanjaro guide had been mature: *pole pole* or slowly is the mantra on the mountain, because the goal is not just to arrive but to arrive safely. At the Everest Base Camp, the young guide who was playing roulette with my water supply once snapped and got mad at me because he felt I wasn't walking fast enough, even after I'd told him that I wasn't taking pills for altitude sickness and needed to slow down. He had decided to punish me somehow for knowing my mind about how I wanted to drink my water.

I think there's a qualitative difference between racism and being raced. Racism, I think, is more sinister and deliberate. But being raced or racing other people is something that people do because they aren't paying attention. It's cultural laziness: we create all these shorthands that allow us to process difference, but a lot of them are focused on the negative rather than the positive. I experience race differently when I'm in countries like Nepal or India, because I get none of the privileges of whiteness. I experience intense scrutiny or unequal treatment from ordinary people who also themselves come from a place where they have no privilege. They have raced me—decided, based on cultural generalisations, who they think I am—in order to process my presence; and, because of the way popular culture from the West especially projects and processes black women, a lot of that is negative. I'm saying "being raced" as a shorthand for a complex intersectionality. Because gender and Africanness is part of the matrix as much as race. That feeling when you walk into a space and you meet people who think that you surely cannot know, just because of who they think you are.

TRAVELLING WHILE BLACK

I don't think I am the kind of African my guide expected. I think he had raced and gendered me, and my showing up a little more sure than he expected me to be frustrated him. Especially when I was hyperventilating and he was struggling to figure out the oxygen, I could tell that his own self-assuredness was falling apart. He needed help, and the only person who could give it was a woman asleep a few rooms over. So I had to struggle for almost thirty minutes before he would go to her for help. When I'd turned out to be different from the way he wanted me to be, he had decided to punish me—which is, of course, dangerous.

I would go back to Nepal in a heartbeat, but I am not sure I would ever attempt Everest Base Camp again. I think the entire experience has become a pipeline for a certain type of thrill-seeking that I only vaguely have a taste for. I love a good challenge, but I hate uncalculated risks, and so much of what is happening on that mountain these days creates a litany of incalculable risks. Later I found out that, while I was struggling up the mountain, a group of more experienced climbers was gearing up to experience the deadliest climbing season in the mountain's history: eleven people died, primarily because the mountain was experiencing its highest level of traffic.

There is so much cruelty and violence in the world that it would be completely absurd, I think, to take myself back to a place where being raced and being unseen nearly cost me my life. I think a lot about how callousness and carelessness can often result in the same outcome. People like to say that, because racism and being raced are different, we should think about the people perpetrating them differently. But for the person on the receiving end, the outcomes are the same. The mind and body still suffer the same. We find ourselves gasping for air. Reciting the alphabet backwards. Willing our bodies and minds not to give in, even though—in a world that keeps us jogging on the treadmill of justifying our right to exist— the only thing we want to do is rest.

15

TERO BURU OF COLLECTIVE GRIEF

Garissa is technically at the edge of Kenya's centre—only five and a half hours from the capital. But this is a country whose imagined geography is shaped more by natural features like Mount Kenya and man-made artefacts like the railway than by physical distances or spatial concepts like "centre". Nairobi, for example, is not in the geographical middle of the country but it is the imagined and functional centre, and so the significance of events is often lazily measured by their proximity to the capital. The railway that connects Kisumu in the west to Mombasa on the east coast separates about the bottom third of the country from the rest, and all of Kenya's major towns lie along this created latitude with the "northern" regions; despite comprising about 57 per cent of the country, these regions are unilaterally thought of as other. Garissa therefore lies at the edge of the beyond, a fictive border town between imagined Kenya, and the Kenya the rest of the country is afraid of and does not want to understand.

About 120,000 people lived in Garissa in 2016, separated from the imagined centre of the country by the mighty Tana River, the longest in Kenya, which rises from a network of tributaries in the south-west before flowing into the Indian Ocean. The massive Tana River is barely navigable and full of crocodiles, and so it functions more as a moat than as a connector. Thus, even though the A3 road that connects Nairobi to Garissa is relatively smooth, perhaps because Garissa is so distant from the railway and on the far riverbank, it may as well be a separate country, for both residents and visitors.

This partly explains why the devastating terrorist attack against Garissa University College in 2015 didn't seem to break as many hearts as the 1998 bombing of the US embassy in Nairobi, or the 2013 attack on the capital's Westgate mall. Maybe this idea that Garissa isn't part of "real" Kenya explains why, one year after the attack on the college, money promised by the government for victim support had been lost to corruption or into a bureaucratic black hole, with no calls for accountability. In a world where sympathy and empathy are predicated on affinity, maybe the underlying idea that Garissa is not technically part of Kenya, or lies just at the edge of it, is the reason why the rest of the country didn't really come together to mourn the senseless loss of life on 2 April 2015. Maybe the spatial dislocation underlies an emotional disconnection between the attack in Garissa and those in the rest of Kenya—and, indeed, the world.

Fear of attack has completely changed the character of Kenya, primarily by exacerbating old tensions and giving them new form. I'm old enough to remember what life was like before we were all afraid. There was a time when you didn't have to get patted down to enter a church or a mosque. I must have taken one of the last flights out of Nairobi where you didn't have to take off your belt, watch and shoes and get your laptop out of your bag before you boarded a plane. This was before Garissa, before Westgate, before Lamu, before Lamu, before Lamu— before all the Lamu attacks. There is a whole generation of adults right now who don't know that there was a time when you could move through the city, and indeed through the world, without being under constant fear, scrutiny and suspicion.

Terrorism has changed the world, and in ways that most of us haven't really thought about properly. Even though experts and laymen are still debating the technicalities—who is a terrorist, who is a criminal and who is a freedom fighter—this wave of mostly young men blowing themselves up in public places has changed the way we occupy space and society. If you were born in the 1970s or 1980s and came of age in the 1990s, you lived through some of the most profound changes the world has ever seen in how it is organised and how individuals are able to use public space. Security has displaced everything else as the main organising principle; so many of our societies have been numbed with grief, intimidated into unquestioningly accepting government directives, and cajoled into hating people because of how they pray. The state has promised us security at a price—the thirty pieces of silver is a measure of our freedom, and for a society like Kenya that has been hit so hard so many times, it has changed how we process grief: whose deaths we mourn and how.

Every community around the world has customs or practices around grief—stages or displays that one is expected to go through in order to signify to the rest of the community that you have been bereaved. In some communities in Italy and Greece, for example, widows wear black indefinitely. Amongst the Banyala of Western Kenya, when the head of a household dies, those who survive him participate in a sombre ceremony in which everyone in the household—men, women and children alike—are shaved bald using a razor blade. The Luo, also of Western Kenya, are renowned for *tero buru*: an elaborate mourning ritual featuring song, dance and traditional liquor. There are often paid, professional mourners, who amplify the sense of loss in order to expand the personality of the deceased after their death, reminding those who are left behind that a good person has passed and that they must be escorted into the afterlife with all the pomp necessary.

The rites vary but the underlying idea is the same: grief is both individual and communal, and those who grieve must go through certain public processes in order to signal and make peace with their loss. Many modern societies have condensed these practices, particularly around funerals; in much of the world people wear black or white to tell the world that someone has passed. *Tero buru* is for those of us who are left behind: a cognitive break between loss and coming to terms with it, to acknowledge that the world is lamenting something important.

But the *tero buru* of terror remains poorly defined. How do you mourn when the scale of devastation is so difficult that we will still be sorting through what is left years after the event? What kind of public display will adequately capture the devastation and confusion of an attack on a dormitory full of teenagers who had their entire lives ahead of them? How can you sit in grief when the source of that grief is so unexpected, so vast and so complete? How can you signal that you are processing something when it affects everything, but you still can't properly define how?

When the news of the 2013 Boston Marathon bombings first emerged, I was walking through the lobby of the law school buildings like hundreds of other students. There was a Patriots and marathon day celebration—an event organised on campus in part to help very stressed-out law school students to relax. But now the gathering was having the opposite effect. We all stood before the screens, confused as to what was happening, wondering what this meant for people we knew or had heard of who were running the marathon. As the reality of the attack unfolded, there was a growing sense of confusion and fear. The bubble that we as students construct around ourselves, in a city of fifty-three universities and colleges, had been breached; exams and deadlines were no longer the most important thing in the world.

After confusion came fear and, in this fear, we were reminded of the nature of difference. Yes, we were all afraid, but we were all afraid of different things. I'm certain that almost everyone was afraid of what this meant for their personal security. But those of us who had experienced violence found themselves struggling with memory and trauma. I suffered severe flashbacks to the Nairobi attacks in 1998, and that sense of violation that comes from having your illusion of safety so violently shattered. My Muslim friends were afraid of the effect that this would have on the already intense scrutiny, discrimination and xenophobia they were enduring. "God," a friend texted, "I hope this person isn't a Muslim. We all do."

In the subsequent hours, like many others in Cambridge, Massachusetts, I was cooped up in my apartment as the police shut down the entire city in pursuit of the surviving bomber. Now that we had a better sense of who the perpetrators were, there was a palpable sense of relief amongst the many sub-communities of my non-white and non-American friends. He was a Muslim man raced white, far down on the list of likely suspects. It's not one of us; thank God. Thank God that a person whose job it is to protect us isn't now going to come up with some other humiliation for us to endure in the name of security. Thank God that some misinformed journalist isn't going to have another excuse to paint an entire community with a tarnished brush. Thank God we won't have to endure any more suspicion than we already do.

Except...

It's hard to explain to our white friends what it feels like to not be white in Europe or in America. For a long time, it wasn't lynchings or cross-burnings that we feared, although the world has deteriorated considerably since 2016. We were exhausted by micro-aggressions, teeny-tiny pinpricks of discomfort with the cumulative effect of disorienting us and making us feel uneasy and unwelcome. Many everyday actions—what music you play at your party, how you choose to wear your trousers, whether or not you sport a hoodie—have become loaded. You need to constantly posture in public, a proverbial show of empty hands, so as not to appear threatening to power.

You need to smile in your discomfort, remain calm in your unease, so as not to draw unnecessary suspicion. Some years ago I was flying to Senegal from New York, and I had the odd experience of having a transport security official grab my (small) braided ponytail. I had just gone through the X-Ray scanner, so I thought I was fine, but she didn't even stop me or try to get my attention. She just grabbed my ponytail and patted it down without so much as an "excuse me". I wanted to go back and complain to her supervisor. My friend reminded me that I was in America now; this was normal, and complaining wouldn't really change anything. This is what it means to be raced.

Edward Said refers to "communities of interpretation" within which labels are created and populated with meaning. At the core of how a community grieves an act of terror is its community of interpretation: the signals and codes that have been developed to signify bereavement. When it comes to terror in the West, the community of interpretation demands retribution as part of the process of mourning: someone has to pay, and usually that someone is an entire group. For those of us who have been raced, part of this is an anxiety that one person's violence will lead to vilification of everyone else. The fact that one Nigerian with a bomb in his shoe means we all have to take our shoes off when we board a plane; but the knowledge that, no matter how many white men wielding semi-automatic weapons destroy people's lives in a matter of seconds, there will never be that collective vilification for them. It's the feeling of exasperation, when a new attack happens, that the list has just grown longer; that there will be a new hoop we must jump through in order to prove to power that we are "respectable black people" or "good Muslims". It's a sense that someone is going to change the tune, just after you'd learnt the dance.

Part of what we mourn when our societies are devastated by terror, even when we have no direct connection to the affected community, is the transformation of some element of ourselves; of how we view the world and how the world views us. We all come into the world as children, with a measure of naivety that gets progressively whittled down, but terror destroys that innocence rapidly. We lose a sense of confidence in the way we experience the world.

* * *

There is no collectively agreed upon method of mourning victims of terror. Part of the challenge is of course that we haven't settled on a definition of what terror is. It is one of those things that you know when you experience it—when you can no longer be around fireworks, or when your heart picks up the pace every time you see a bald white man covered in tattoos. Powerful nations want us to accept their definition of political terror—violence carried out with the intention of spreading fear amongst society—but because it is so fluid, we expand it to include our own types of terror. Gendered violence is terror for 51 per cent of the world's population. For some, terror is bombs falling indiscriminately on civilian populations. For others, it is police officers targeting poor young men for arrest or shooting. But there is reluctance to accept this definition; so, when we say "terrorism", we are mostly referring to violence inflicted in pursuit of specific political ideologies.

This belaboured definition is perhaps why we don't see the suffering of the people most likely to be victims of terror attacks.

We don't mourn everyone's tragedy equally, and the hierarchy reflects the biases that we individually and collectively hold. In Western countries there will be promises, memorials, full-page spreads and thirty articles explaining in great detail who the victims were, what they were doing when they died and how the people they loved will be affected now that they have been left behind. Particularly where most of the victims are white and the perpetrator of the terror is not, there must be public performances of grief.

But there are no monuments or memorials to the hundreds of thousands of Iraqis, Afghanis, Somalis and others who are on the frontline of terror's violence. There is far less acknowledgement of sadness when most of the victims are brown or black, even if they are in the West. They die anonymously and collectively, and even in death are deprived of the full spectrum of our grief, because they carry the shroud of suspicion with them. When a bomb goes off in Mogadishu, there will inevitably be people online saying openly in comment forums that the Somalis "bring this on themselves".

Kenya sits at an in-between of this pattern. The us-versus-them dynamic between the population living along or south of the railway line—*watu wa reli*, the people of the railway—and the marginalised people of the imagined north creates a cognitive dissonance that undermines the national capacity for empathy. The Kenyan government fought for years to gain and keep political control over the northern regions, but once they had it, they had no idea what to do with it. When you go to Garissa, Wajir or Mandera, people ask you, "How is Kenya?" This affects how ordinary Kenyans, in their casual conversations and in the press, do or don't process the depth of suffering from terrorism and its by-products in these northern societies. It affects how we mourn their victims of terror.

Since the rise of the terrorist group Al Shabaab in the early 2000s, civilians in the north-east of the country, all the way down to Lamu, have been the majority victims. Buses taking people home for the holidays and compounds where teachers congregate have been attacked. Miners have been rounded up and killed. And, on that cold April morning in 2015, hundreds of university students in Garissa, many of whose families had sold, bartered and traded everything to give their children a chance at a better life, were exterminated in an hours-long orgy of violence and cruelty.

But, instead of sitting in the discomfort of our shared grief, the government has resorted to criminalising the people who are most likely to be victims. Arbitrary arrests abound. Young people have been killed and disappeared by police who are putatively sent to protect them. Entire towns in the north have been placed under inhumane curfews—measures that would be unacceptable in other parts of the country—simply because our imagined geography says that it's "us against them". Significantly, Kenya has imported from the United States and its rhetoric on the war on terror an unhealthy fear of the 30 per cent of our population that is Muslim, and this Islamophobia—ironically championed by many Muslims in government—has slowly but surely been incorporated into the way we process terror and how we must be seen to respond to it publicly. Punishing those who are most likely to be victims has become part of our mourning ritual.

For the individual Kenyan, reacting to terror has become a choice between public and emphatic displays of patriotism, or being accused of sympathising with the attackers. We are told, rather unsubtly, that blind support for the government and the military is the only way to distinguish Us from Them, that this is the only acceptable way to display our grief. If you ask questions or demand accountability from the government, you are not patriotic enough. A conspiracy of silence designed to shield the state from accountability is ultimately diluting our capacity to process the full reality of terror and what it does to the individual and society. And it is keeping those of us living near the centre of power at arm's length from those whose voices struggle to carry here. We are pressured to publicly acknowledge attacks or face criticism. But in the same breath we are discouraged from mourning victims as individuals, and instead invited to mourn the assault against the commons. Victims of terror are no longer people with families and histories, but totems: symbols that we must acknowledge even if we don't fully understand why. Because, as much as this was a thing that happened to all of us, it is not a thing of which we are allowed to have an individual experience. Our cues on the proper way to grieve must come from the state.

Social media has relieved some of this baggage, but has made it heavier in other ways. It allows people to build a sense of community or solidarity, but it also makes grief more performative than organic. True grief serves an important purpose, but online the process becomes the goal: we have to tell everyone that we are sad. It's no coincidence that these superficial and abstract forms of "mourning" are taking place in a space outside and beyond any real place we might call home. It becomes a contest entirely removed from the people or places that have actually suffered the loss. *You* may just have tweeted the hashtag, but *I* changed my profile picture and added a flag to my banner. Well, *I* changed my *name* to the hashtag. You may have worn black for a month, but I shaved my scalp entirely.

The attack in Garissa triggered many of these responses. The hashtag #147NotJustANumber was created in order to allow public grieving and create a community of accountability, as the Kenyan government's cover-up machine already seemed in motion. "Not just a number" created an archive of sorrow, fleshing out stories to give each victim some of the colour and richness that made them human—because thinking about death in the aggregate tends to overwhelm, and makes smaller gestures of grief seem trite. Does leaving a single rose at a site where 200 have died even matter? How about a teddy bear? At the same time, social media is unrooted, by nature a transient space. You cannot wear black on social media forever. Things are designed to trend for a season at most before they are dislodged by something else. Garissa showed us that the *tero buru* of public grief over terrorist attacks may be swift, but is not necessarily deep or permanent, because of what these spaces have done to our attention spans and interest levels. Add that to the permanent lack of interest in places like Garissa, on the imaginative periphery, and there is almost no chance of a meaningful mourning process.

Victims of terror are still people, and they leave people behind. When death comes unexpectedly and brutally, grief can take months or even years to settle in completely. People might look fine on the outside, while their minds and hearts are struggling to come to terms with what has happened to their sense of home. Now amplify this by hundreds and thousands of people every day, dying violent and unnecessary deaths away from the glare of the international press. Imagine what it must be like to live in a society where death comes so suddenly that it must happen without grief, because you never even have time to process it before the next attack hits.

What happens when our public performance of grief is so removed from the physical site of the grief that it leads to the dehumanisation of the people there who have actually lost their loved ones? When 147 people are killed in a small town, but the grief of the town is lost in security operations, where does that grief settle? These are people who have lost not their sense of safety, but their children. How do we translate our alarm into tangible action on their behalf? What happens to the people who are left behind when the rest of us stop performing our rituals of grief?

These are the questions that Kenya has not answered for Garissa. There was public grief. Anger, chastisement, promises of retribution—and then silence. For a year, those who were most affected—those who lost family members and those who watched their students and charges die—were completely abandoned. Because this was an attack that happened in the peri-Kenya; at the margins of the imagination of what Kenya is, and because "those people" only get a small measure of our sadness. It's hard enough to get a sense of state accountability for victims of terror in Nairobi. For people who live in the peri-Kenya, their grief and sorrow has been compounded by systemic neglect, enabled by the inattention of *watu wa reli*, the people of the railway.

In Garissa, after the hashtags came a deep systemic abandonment, where the *tero buru* was supplanted by the practical concerns of surviving a predatory state. Money allocated for funerals, or for counselling and scholarships for survivors, has disappeared in the government bureaucracy. For many families, the children who were murdered had been the first in their family to attend university, and they had relied on wages from work/study initiatives in the community—many paying better than full-time jobs elsewhere—to support family incomes. These deaths have had practical consequences, leading to the death of at least one parent, attributed to depression. Even the one-year anniversary event, planned by the university as an intimate commemoration of personal or immediate grief, was hijacked for political gain, with local politicians who had only once visited the university after the attack jostling in the background for pride of place as mourner-in-chief until late into the night. This fleeting attention only served to prove more than ever that, for Kenya, Garissa is of marginal consequence.

The town has been hollowed out by the mass exit of non-local students, not just at the University College but across all four institutions of higher learning in Garissa. The loss of these students, who were integral not just to the university but also to the community—as teacher trainees, clerks and other valuable entry-level employees—is biting. And yet the story of the human tragedy has been captured by security discourse, erasing in the process the real suffering of a community that took in terrified students and helped collect battered bodies that had begun to decompose in the blistering sun during the twenty-hour siege. The communal and personal grief remains suspended, waiting for room to be expressed, much like the unshed tears that glisten in the eyes of residents when they are given room to speak about the attack. Do people from the peri-Kenya get to be devastated by the loss, or must they continue to quietly navigate their compounded tragedy—of being at the periphery of a country already at the periphery of the global imagination?

After 2001's September 11 attack in the United States, which remains one of history's most devastating, terms were set for public articulation of grief after terror. Aside from public mourning, there was the promise to "never forget", the military response, the memorialisation of each individual who had been lost. But when the grief is in faraway places, the terms remain partial and unarticulated. Does *The New York Times* owe every single victim of a terror attack in Mogadishu a face, a name, a time of death and a small moment of collective grief? Maybe. Some would say maybe not—that that is the work of the Somali newspapers. *The New York Times* is an American newspaper facing primarily American audiences. But instead of "never forget", the lack of focus on those who've been lost sends an unsubtle message of "we must move on". Whose job is it to tell us that the people who have died were just ordinary people going about their business? In newspapers like these—facing a powerful domestic audience, but craving international acclaim—black and brown people don't get the full contemporary rites and rituals of mourning terror victims, a proper *tero buru*.

Sometimes the main obstacle to these processes is the state itself. In Kenya, the government wants to maintain a monopoly on public grief and discourages such recognition of the victims of terror. It wants us to move on, but won't answer questions that would help people to do that. It doesn't acknowledge how many people were killed or how they died, and this too is about who is considered a "real person" and where is considered a "real place" in the age of terror. It denies black and brown mourners the chance to grieve terror outside of the security narrative. In the name of that security, it never tells us what happened before, during or after the attack, so we never know what we can do better. All we know is that, when it is ready, the state will snatch away the freedom of our own land. We will be banned from taking photographs in our cities, frisked before we enter our churches, followed and threatened by policemen on our streets, rounded up and taken from them, and detained in underground cages at the largest sports stadium in the country—because of security.

The story of the Garissa attack has become simply the story of Al Shabaab and the Kenya Defence Forces, not of the teachers who spent an entire week identifying the bodies of students they had loved and counselled. Sadness is no longer the privilege of those who grieve, but of the leaders at all levels who instrumentalise our grief for political ends. The tragedy of terrorism in Kenya is not framed as a loss of life, but as a loss of income through falling tourist numbers. Internationally, it is one amongst a litany of attacks that proves how volatile and unsafe Africa is, not a crisis that has undone a community where people lived and loved.

In January 2016, when Al Shabaab overran a Kenyan military base at El Adde, Somalia, the government in Nairobi refused to comment publicly or to acknowledge the dead. Only a lapse from the Somali president during a television interview told us that 200 young men had been killed. Two hundred sons, fathers and brothers who were never coming home. But their own government, which had sent them to the frontline to face the terror group, would not even give the country they were supposed to defend a chance to mourn them. Kenya believes that acknowledging victims of terror deprives them of their power, and so, even as the attacks intensify, so does the silence around them. But what power did they even have in life, as prisoners of their geography?

Is a *tero buru* of terror that focuses on and acknowledges loss and suffering, all around the world and in every corner of a country, possible? Can we be equally sad about all the victims of terror in the world, given how many there are and how the numbers keep growing? Can the human brain—individually and collectively—process such an enormous thing? Will it ever be possible for someone in New York to be as devastated by a terrorist attack in Baghdad or Mogadishu as they are by one in London or Paris? Or for a native of Nairobi to feel as deeply an attack in peri-Kenya as they would one on their own doorstep?

It seems difficult to imagine, but cultures of mourning are shaped over time, when we express discomfort with one trajectory and push for things to move in a different direction. There is more awareness now than ever that deaths of certain people from certain places invite greater public grief than others, and that this is because of the hierarchies we have created, which are inherently unjust. There are more calls than ever before to mourn alongside the victims of terror, wherever they may be, because we have a greater awareness of shared humanity. What transnational *tero buru* will emerge from this remains to be seen. Anyone who has ever lost a loved one knows that there is no single correct formula for expressing sadness. There is just sadness. There is just the slow realisation that the person who made you laugh, who kept you up late on the phone just to hear your voice, who called you by that nickname that made you smile, is never coming back.

Tero buru, when all is said and done, is a performance that may never correspond to the grief of those who perform it. But perhaps the *tero buru* of collective mourning for victims of terror is still developing and up for debate. Maybe our hashtags and profile pictures will evolve into actual actions taken in solidarity: school fees and medical bills paid, memorial ceremonies, pushes for policy change. Perhaps the lesson five years on in Garissa—abandoned domestically and internationally, separated from the rest of Kenya by an imagined distance that is actually very easy to overcome—is that the real measure of our grief shouldn't be in how loudly and heavily we beat our chests, but in everything that happens after the ceremonies are over. Perhaps the *tero buru* will ring hollow until we learn to acknowledge the completeness of the places lying at the periphery of our own imagination: to travel there and walk with the people, physically or psychologically.

16

OH, THE PLACES YOU'LL PEE!

"But where do you pee?"

It's an honest and genuine question for the woman backpacker in a world where many seemingly rational adult men genuinely believe that women don't need to eliminate waste. The idea that we must be genteel and even a little cloistered from the vagaries of budget travel is pretty pervasive. And stupid. Look, as long as you're a part of this species, you're going to need to eat and drink, and get rid of the by-products of those processes. Deal with it.

The sheer volume of women I've met who opt out of backpacking as a way of seeing the world because they cannot fathom peeing anywhere that isn't a porcelain throne is heartbreaking. It closes off so much of the world! The sad reality is that globally running water and indoor plumbing are a luxury, and for the vast majority of people in the world, the idea of a toilet is strange. And part of the idea behind backpacking is that we make ourselves and our needs so small that we are able to make room for the grandest adventures. So to get to some of the more interesting parts of the world—to watch the sunrise from the top of Mount Kenya, or visit the secret beaches of Northern Madagascar—you and your nervous bladder will just have to make it work.

I absolutely get it. It's one of the hardest adjustments to make to life on the road. It's one thing to get used to surviving on bread, yoghurt and water—it's another thing altogether to coerce a shy bladder to let loose over a garbage heap. Those of us who are socialised around modern conveniences aren't just going to give them up, least of all people like those I grew up with, who are mostly one or two generations out from having to use the bush or a shoddily constructed pit latrine. Who would choose to go back to that, when Japan is inventing toilets that work with a remote control?

I remember exactly where I was when the switch flipped for me. I was in Lomé, the Togolese capital, on my first major trip in Africa outside my home country. The highlight of city life in Lomé is a street called Brochettes sur la capitale—rows and rows of roast beef, chicken and even rabbit skewers served by frantic men in multi-coloured two-piece suits, backed by a thumping soundtrack of West African dance music. The skewers were delicious and the drink flowed freely, and because the drink flowed freely, the inevitable happened. I needed to go.

You must understand that Togo is one of the poorest countries in the world. Running water is scarce. I'm not sure what I was expecting, but I can assure you it's not what I got. Who would expect a full porcelain toilet mounted over a pit latrine, with no piping and no running water? A metaphor, perhaps, for Togo itself—odd bits of contemporary amenities grafted onto deep histories and choking on rotten politics. But great metaphors make terrible toilets. I walked in, encountered the stench, then turned around and walked right back out. And then I remembered that I really, really had to go. What could I do?

This was the moment I discovered that switch somewhere in our minds: the one that allows us all to turn off unpleasantness when there is business to be handled. It's entirely possible to choose not to notice something vile or not to make a fuss when you genuinely have no choices. If you can just flip this switch for a couple of minutes, the list of places that "you just can't go" shrinks exponentially. For me, the world of long-distance bus travel opened up, and I've never looked back.

Finding this switch means that, on a thirty-six-hour bus ride from Malawi into Tanzania, when the bus breaks down in a two-horse town with no bar or hotel, you don't panic. It means that when you ask for a toilet in Madagascar, and the waitress in the small rest stop in a small town outside a small town outside a small town points to the garbage heap, you roll with it. It means that when your guide gestures to a bush on the side of the trail in the Abedares and adds, "Look out for elephants," you can laugh instead of panic.

It's not all champagne and roses, of course. Budget travel is much kinder to cis men than to anyone else. There is no feminist solution yet to the fact that men can pee just about anywhere, because the process isn't as exposing for them as it is for us. They annoyingly just don't seem to need or value privacy the way we do. Standing in the middle of the Danakil Depression in Ethiopia—endless miles of salt plains with nary a tree in sight—desperately needing to go, you start to wonder if this a new feminist frontier. Out in the desert in Sudan, when your driver says, "Go behind the car, I promise I won't look," you may find yourself genuinely working through the mechanics of peeing in a bottle.

Then you go, and the crisis is averted, and you go back to the more important business of marvelling at that glorious desert sunset.

17

ON RACE

The only time someone has ever called me "n****r" to my face was on a subway in Manhattan, just by Times Square. Neither I nor my friends were ready for it. The older white lady in the black fur coat and starched, high-waisted blue jeans was asking for money. She asked my friends first, and they told her they didn't have any, and we held our breath because one of those friends was a hijabi and this was the USA after September 11. But she said nothing to my friend. Only when I said no, and as she walked away into the subway, did she say loudly and directly to me, "Oh, what do you know? You're just a n****r anyway."

I don't know how to describe in succinct terms what that word feels like. I can tell you what it sounds like—the bitterness in the "n" and the angry "g", doubled up to emphasise the ugliness in the heart of the person who uses it, casually spat but designed to burn through the skin like acid. I can explain to you how it sears through your spirit, how when I think about this incident my ears still faintly ring with rage and also a measure of humiliation. Humiliation because there is no other word in the English language that can carry with it the same weight of centuries of systematic violence, deliberate cruelty, venomous derision and arbitrary assault. The only words that come even close are other words that white power screamed over black bodies to the same effect in other parts of the world—kaffir, untouchable.

You run through every variation of speaking up for yourself in rapid fire—I'm not sure every cell in my body has ever worked so quickly to try and think of anything I could say that would mean something, in the fog of rage and hatred that was coursing through my own body. Who does she think she is? I am smart. I am educated. I am worthy. In retrospect, after years of being bombarded with videos of black people in the USA stomped on, shot at, spat at, beaten down and degraded by white people, I realise now that I was lucky she just walked away. By the time the ringing in my ears had gone down a decibel or two—at least low enough for me to think of something quippy and searing to say or do—all I could see was the black fur weaving through the crowded subway car, and not the wrong end of a gun.

There is nothing a black person can say to a racist that can even come close to what that word does to us. This is a word that was created specifically to crush the spirit of the person who heard it: it was created to be the vocal articulation of a system of violence. And so when you hear it said to you, there's anger, frustration and humiliation, because there is almost nothing you can do to defend yourself against its weight. There is nothing you can say back that will have the same effect as the thing you just heard.

It's not an exaggeration to say that hearing that word from a white person's lips is a deeply harrowing experience. If you know your history, it makes you think about everyone who heard it before you, and what came next, in a not-so-distant time when young men in the Congo could have their arms cut off for not tapping enough rubber, or young black women could be turned into permanent sexual slaves. I hear that word and I remember taking a knee in the dungeons at Elmina Castle in Ghana, where slaves were held before they were sent off to the New World—a dank, desolate place that still smells like oppression. A single word that threatens unspeakable violence, and demands that the hearer do something—anything—but what? Do you punch? Do you yell back? Do you shoot? What can you actually do when someone picks up the entire weight of an ugly violent history, condenses it and wields it as a weapon?

* * *

My time in the US taught me to sit in the discomfort of racism, which followed me around more overtly and unabashedly there than it has just about everywhere else in the world. It's not that I had never experienced racism or thought about it before I moved to America. I think it's more that, in other contexts, people make the effort to pretend that it's about something else. I am a product of Nairobi: a city steeped in an apartheid legacy that still draws invisible lines across society, dictating who can marry whom, who can socialise with whom, who can buy an apartment or a house from whom. And I had, by the time I moved to the US, also lived in Europe. In the UK's West Midlands, where in my first week there were race riots in Birmingham that left two people dead: mistrust between the black and Asian communities in Britain's biggest city after London was imprinted even while the university operated as if it were wholly separate from the troubles at its doorstep.

But there is just something about the complete lack of shame with which the US wields its racism that forces you, as the non-white person, to develop a cognitive architecture to understand it, to buttress your consciousness so you can survive. It's not that it's worse; it's just unapologetic. James Baldwin once wrote that "to be black and conscious in America is to be in a constant state of rage". You have to not only live with that rage but manage it so that it doesn't devour you. You can't privilege your way out of US racism, so it confronts you everywhere you turn—from the subways of Manhattan to the hallways of Harvard. In Africa, and in Europe to some extent, we who are middle-class or rich often buy some mitigation out of the worst of racism, but in the US you can never be rich enough or powerful enough to run away from the logic of a country that is determined to reject you.

At the same time, in Africa where the majority of the population is black, race comes to you jumbled up with so many other forms of systemic violence and exclusion that it can be difficult to parse the source of the needle pricking your conscience. Is this white man at the golf club in this wealthy suburb of Nairobi speaking to me this way because I'm black, because I don't look rich, or because I'm a woman? Is the gallerist in Cape Town following us around as we take in the paintings because we have dark skin and defiant afros, or because we are in flip-flops so she doesn't think we could possibly afford any of the art on the walls? Did this Indian Kenyan man invite our mutual white friend to his party but not me because I am from a different social class, or because I'm black? When racialism comes to you with such ambiguity, it can be difficult to work through your own reaction to it. Especially in a context where you are told that you are free—that you have the freedom your ancestors fought for—experiencing race can be a deeply disorienting experience.

Travel has given me the tools to think about race in more articulate terms. The dislocation of mobility—of not having the pre-set crutches that we rely upon to navigate the places we call home—allows me to be bolder and more direct in calling out racism when I see it. Some famous writers have gotten in trouble for saying that they never realised they were black until they left Africa. I think that's a clumsy way to describe something that is true for most Africans, who move from being in black-majority societies to black-minority societies. It's not that black people don't experience racism in Africa; more that most of us are cognitively reluctant to attribute what we experience on the continent as racism, because it defies the central logic that orders our lives in Africa—that flicker of faith that, at least in Africa, we are free. How can we be free if the malaise that tortured and killed our grandparents is still with us? How can we live in a reality in which we failed to fulfil the promise of Uhuru?

Travel, and working in and around issues of migration, have given me the vocabulary I needed to begin to name the beast. Specifically, backpacking, which depends much more on immersing yourself in local culture to survive than travelling around five-star resorts in air-conditioned land cruisers. When your possessions are distilled to the most essential, your connections are necessarily fleeting, and your interactions occur in hyper-speed; you begin to see things in Technicolor. You process experiences with a lot less qualification, in part because you don't have to pretend to keep getting along with people you are never going to see again. But then again, those of us who are travelling by choice have an even more privileged experience—our money gives us further protection from the disorientation and the pushback that may come our way. It's not an absolute protection, as I was reminded that day in Manhattan—but millions of people around the world have had even that taken away from them, as they leave everything behind, and try to enter a new society.

Since I began backpacking, I've spent a lot of my time in contexts where I've been expected to pretend not to notice race. As a tourist in my own country, there are many hotels that still openly treat their black guests as second-class. At university working on refugee and migration studies, the R word was taboo, and you had to provide the most complex theoretical justifications as to why a state would exclude thousands of people, possibly condemning them to a watery grave, without using the word "racism". I once worked for an international organisation working primarily in Africa that recruited two black women as part of a cohort of eighteen, then promptly promoted everyone in the cohort to permanent staff except the two of us. In all of this the expectation was that I must silently bear the indignities and humiliation, continue to work twice as hard and get half as far, for whatever morsels might fall from the table.

I never could, and I notice with mild amusement how uncomfortable it makes people who benefit from racial privilege to name the thing. Especially around people who think they are good and "not racist", naming the thing is a powerful taboo. But how can you pretend not to notice something that is so obvious and pertinent? When you feel the weight of something so keenly, but the world around you forces you to pretend that it doesn't matter or even doesn't exist, you spend a lot of time inside your head testing the weight of your experiences; feeling around the soft contours of this hard, heavy thing.

Race and racism, I find, are not necessarily conjoined things. Other people have written more deeply and more eloquently about this, but I think racism is a function of choice: an active decision to instrumentalise an aspect of a person's identity against them. Racism is violence. Racism begins with a decision not to see a person beyond the body, and often culminates in actions to force that person to shrink back into those presumptions. Naming the thing—identifying the sequence of steps that begin with the decision and culminate in the action—is an important part of fighting against it, even if it makes the genteel uncomfortable.

"You're just a n****r, anyway". My heart still skips a few beats whenever I replay those moments in my head. Time slows down, and I see her every gesture and motion and start to think of all the things I could have said to take back even a measure of power from that moment. Like most people, my first instinct is to argue the point. I'm not *just* anything. I am a sister, a daughter, a friend, a partner, a writer, a thinker—here is a long list of ineffable qualifications to prove to you that I am not *just* anything. I am singular. I am unique. I am an integral part of the tapestry of the world and the world cannot function without me. It's a tantalising prospect, but the older I get the more I realise how wasteful and futile it is to debate your humanity with someone who doesn't want to see it. The point for the racist, I think, is that you are not a person. You are a character that they have invented to play a specific role in the script they have created about their lives, and you can't argue your way out of hate.

* * *

I think about this more broadly in the work that I have done on migration and human rights. I think about all those people who have walked across the desert and braved slave camps and the purest distillates of hate to show up in Europe, only to be cast into the role of an existential threat to the very survival of European "culture". However many hundreds of years of culture, erased by a few hundred people trying to be safe. The way we've framed the discussion of human mobility focuses on the bodies and the physical presence of those who move, not the stories and the complexities behind them. And particularly people who can't buy their way into our attention. If you have money, people are likely to be more generous with the way they interpret your presence. But if you don't, plenty of people will stop at the baggage and label that they have in mind for you, and often that is based on the imagined threat you pose, and on keeping you out as integral to their survival.

We spend so much of our lives making presumptions about other people and navigating other people's presumptions about ourselves that we often don't notice we are doing it. But this intellectual laziness is one of the first things that human mobility strikes against. It wasn't until I began to journey beyond my horizons that I began to question everything. I grew up in a strict, rules-based society where the constructed British canon of bearded white male writers, plus Achebe, Soyinka and the occasional Enid Blyton, was the standard for good writing. We might read black women writers, but we didn't revere them. In writing as in travel, they were marginal and their stories tertiary—not even secondary.

By the time I was in high school, I had a vision of Africa that was painted by a European hand. I learnt to be ashamed of African poverty, about how we lacked a history before the Europeans arrived, about how the introduction of Friesian cattle forever changed the landscape of dairy farming in Kenya and led to "development". I believed in the superiority of the English language, and whenever people asked how many languages I spoke, I always said one or two (English and Kiswahili), having internalised the illegitimacy of my mother tongue. I'm ashamed to admit that I was even afraid of Africa: the Africans of CNN, warring Africans who killed each other on a whim, who hated women and did violence to them, who ate monkeys and spread Ebola, whose bodies were ravaged with AIDS, and who were always waiting to steal from each other.

Travelling allowed me to reflect on how my society had chosen to situate itself, and to wonder who I was outside these simple rules that I had inherited and was still being fed by Western perspectives. Who could I be if I chose not to be "good"? Who was I when all I had to rely on was a simple grasp of the language and a need to get home before sunset? Who was I, when I wasn't reading from the script that my community had written for me? That to me has been the role of travel. Without it, I would have continued moving through the world with the assumption I knew things that I simply did not.

When someone enters your society and you have no previous experience of their culture or their history, you want to quickly put them in a box—any box—so that you can move past the challenge of having to encounter them as a human being with a unique life arc. You don't want to speak to Anita from Rwanda. You want to assemble as many tropes or presumptions together as you can, so that Anita can be the archetype for Rwandans. We don't want to do the work, and it is work, of having a human encounter that is riddled with complexity and nuance. So we reach for the stereotypes, for most of us formed and informed by popular culture.

Travel and migration are qualitatively different experiences, united by the thread of mobility and disconnection. We disconnect ourselves from the familiar, for whatever reason and enter the unfamiliar. But the things that make us leave, and the expectations of how we will be treated when we arrive, are qualitatively different for the migrant and the traveller. The traveller enters the new society with an expectation that they will be treated decently, at the very least because of the money they are bringing into the economy. But the refugee or migrant who has left everything else behind for the prospect of safety often arrives tentative and afraid, their survival hinging on the kindness of the society that they enter. These varying degrees of entitlement shift the demands that we make on the new society, even if the disconnect and the discomfort are the same.

All of which is to say that the black traveller and the black migrant do not have identical experiences, but the black traveller is living in microcosm the story of the black migrant; the black traveller and the black migrant have resonating appreciation for the burdens of race. Mobility produces a reaction in the society that you enter, as it does in yourself, even if the difference is that the traveller has chosen to enter and has a set schedule to leave, while the migrant is in search of something more permanent. More importantly, the way in which a society treats visiting travellers can reveal a lot about how it will eventually treat migrants and refugees. My own experience of travel has given a great deal of urgency to the work that I have done protecting the rights of refugees and migrants, precisely because it resonates so keenly with the fleeting but cutting experiences of structural and physical violence that I have survived.

* * *

But travel has also taught me that a different way is possible. My time in Gorom-Gorom, the market town in northern Burkina Faso that we visited in Chapter 2, was the first time that I had backpacked alone, having left Togo and Ghana as part of a student group. Initially, the plan was to remain in Ouagadougou, the glorious capital, but Burkina Faso is the kind of place that pries your heart open, insinuates itself into every crevice, and demands that your brain satisfy its curiosity about how such a singular place could possibly exist. At the crossroads where the Sahara becomes the Sahel, it is a stifling hot, landlocked country hemmed in by massive dunes in the north and humid clusters of green in the South. Most importantly, it is a country that lives up to its name: Burkina Faso, the land of honest men.

On the bus from Accra in Ghana to Ouagadougou, I sat next to an older woman in a traditional African print dress, and behind a young man in khakis and wire-rimmed glasses. At first, my plan was to say nothing, because my French wasn't that good and I didn't want to give over that I was a foreigner. I was alone, and I was afraid. But it was a 26-hour drive from Accra, and eventually they wore me down. When they heard I was a Kenyan, they couldn't believe it: "I've never met a Kenyan before!" the woman exclaimed excitedly. And I had never met anyone who was excited to meet a Kenyan before—at least, no one who wasn't a Kenyan abroad themselves.

These two strangers would be the starting point of a spectacular experience for me of welcoming and belonging. The entire time I was in Ouagadougou, they fed me, they showed me around, they asked after my well-being. They helped me navigate a country I had never set foot in before, and asked for nothing in return, even when I insisted. "We just want you to feel welcome," they would say, and the three of us frequently made an odd trio in Ouagadougou's markets and museums.

Those early days gave me the courage to venture further into Burkina Faso, and so I bought a bus ticket—from Ouagadougou to Dori, and then in the back of an open truck from Dori to Gorom-Gorom. The guide book said that the Thursday market at Gorom-Gorom had been running longer than anyone could remember. It brought together traders from all across the Sahara and the Sahel, bringing salt, gold, indigo-dyed fabric and lately plastic homewares and stainless steel kitchenware. It was a once-in-a-lifetime experience, they said, and I was instantly sold, in part because I had already been made welcome in Burkina Faso.

And once in a lifetime it was. The local hotel at Gorom-Gorom was under renovation, so instead I rented a room from the Catholic mission staffed by one priest from the south. On Wednesday evening, I couldn't get any of the moto taxis in the town centre to agree to drive me out to the desert to watch the sunrise, and I was disappointed. But when the priest heard that I had come such a long way and risked leaving without achieving that singular goal, he fuelled his motorcycle and took me himself, and I watched my first sunrise over the Sahara.

What I experienced in Burkina Faso was a community that saw the traveller and the migrant not as a threat but as an opportunity—and not just an economic opportunity but as a person who brought something interesting and unique into society. I entered a place where no one wanted anything from me, other than for me to experience the best of their society. I saw a paradigm that the textbooks on migration want us to believe doesn't happen: there were societies that still saw the traveller as a welcome addition and not as a burden to be avoided. It forced me to reconsider so many of the things that my formal education had taught me were inevitable. I could no longer accept that, because West and East have decided to withdraw behind walls and fortresses to exclude the Other, the rest of us are obligated to follow suit because that is what "progress" or modernity demands.

I saw on that first backpacking trip something that I think needs to be protected, and the more I travel and work in this space the more vulnerable I realise it is. An approach to receiving the traveller or the migrant that isn't contingent on money, but is predicated on empathy, kindness and recognising that mobility rubs the soul a little raw, can be a political praxis for dealing with the politics of mobility.

The experience of travelling while black—either as a voyager, as a migrant, or as a refugee—is united by this narrow thread of a soul rubbed raw from the disorientation of leaving what is familiar behind. Someone travelling for leisure can, depending on their budget, pay their way out of some of the discomfort that a hostile receiving community might project. Migrants and refugees have no such choice. The fact of human mobility isn't going anywhere any time soon, so it remains on us to articulate a shift towards responding to people on the move with empathy. Desert communities across the Sahara and the Middle East understood the burdens that disorientation can place on the soul, and have traditions of welcoming the traveller and the migrant. These practices don't have to be quaint or archaic; they can be the status quo.

* * *

Race was an unspoken but really integral part of my experience of Burkina Faso. I think that because African communities can't instantly discount me, a black person, as other, I get a little room to exist as an individual, rather than an archetype for my society. But it isn't always that simple—the fact of blackness isn't enough to create a globally unified community. So much of what black communities learn about each other around the world is filtered through hegemonic media with a distinct interest in preserving racial hierarchies; we often have these crude cultural clashes, battling each other with the stereotypes we've absorbed about one another for far too long. And economic disparities make it difficult for our communities to interact with each other authentically.

The histories of diaspora clashes between African and African American communities could fill an entire volume on their own, but quite simply neither side is speaking to an authentic or even complete version of the other. Social media is helping circumvent some of these difficulties, but for most of us the only version Africans know of African Americans and vice versa is the version we see on CNN, listen to in popular music, or see caricatured on television. This social media moment echoes the moments in the early twentieth century, and again in the 1950s and 1960s, when socio-political leaders deliberately worked together to name anti-black racism as a common enemy and to work together to defeat it. The birth of Pan-Africanism on the continent couldn't have happened without W.E.B. Du Bois and Marcus Garvey; Malcolm X and Maya Angelou's civil rights activism was influenced by the time they spent in Africa. Similarly, Martin Luther King Jr cited a trip to Ghana and Nigeria in 1951, when he was just 31, as a moment when his hopes for the civil rights movement expanded.

"You're just a n****r anyway".

Anti-black racism is a global problem that doesn't make national distinctions, a common enemy that must be named and put in its proper place. It is not an inevitable enemy. No one comes into the world knowing to hate. It is something people are taught. It is a product of decisions followed by actions, designed to create an entire sub-class of people whose exclusion can be handily justified and used as a bogey man for the fears of people who don't want to put in the work and contemplate the humanity of other people. Toni Morrison once observed that there are people in the world who think that they need racism, because without it they may have to confront their own fundamental shortcomings. Racism is ignorance scaffolded by intellectual laziness and bloodlust.

But it also creates an imperative for people to work together against it, because its tentacles are so long and deep in everything. The onus isn't on the victims of racism to prove that they are worthy, but on the rest of us who have a measure of privilege in a deeply unequal and unjust world to make a better way more feasible. We should never feel the need to negotiate or justify our humanity with people who are determined not to see it. We can, however, do our part to dismantle the structures that make such calculated ignorance and violence feasible. Speak up for those that need defending. Connect the dots between the struggles that are grounded in anti-black racism and establish a united front against them. Show up for the resistance. Tell the stories about societies and histories that were organised differently: where the value of a person wasn't measured against the colour of their skin or the depth of their wallet.

I still get angry sometimes when I imagine myself back on that subway carriage, rage roiling inside me and rolling off my skin. I feel petulant with it. I feel frustrated that a single word can reduce me to such impotence and frustration, and that so many millions of people in the world have it so much worse. I think about all the countless ways that a single word can escalate into violence and death overseen by state structures complicit in the humiliation and degradation of black people.

I think of a thread that weaves together the bodies of black men murdered by the police in the US and Brazil; the black and brown migrant workers who were the first to die when COVID-

19 arrived in the UK and Europe; the migrants and refugees that European countries allow to die on the high seas; the exploited underclass in Africa toiling through bloody fingers on plantations and in underground mines to keep the beast of capitalism fed; Asia's unwanted and untouchable. I think of all of these things and the thread that unites them and I get tired. But I refuse to remain paralysed with anger. Travel has taught me that a different world is possible and even attainable, and that, even though the beast is large and its tentacles are long, there are enough of us to do something meaningful towards destroying it.

FURTHER READING

Michel Adam (ed.), *Indian Africa: Minorities of Indian-Pakistani Origin in Eastern Africa* (Mkuki na Nyota, 2015).

Steve Biko, *I Write What I Like* (Heinemann, 1987).

Hélène Charton-Bigot and Deyssi Rodriguez-Torres (Ed), *Nairobi Today: The Paradox of a Fragmented City* (Mkuki wa Nyota, 2010).

Shiraz Durrani, *Kenya's War of Independence: Mau Mau and its Legacy of Resistance to Colonialism and Imperialism, 1948–1990* (Vita Books, 2018).

Caroline Elkins, *Britain's Gulag: The Brutal End of Empire in Kenya* (Pimlico, 2005).

Frantz Fanon, *The Wretched of the Earth* (Penguin Classics, 2001).

Paul Gilroy, *The Black Atlantic: Modernity and Double Consciousness* (Harvard University Press, 1993).

Stuart Hall, *The Fateful Triangle: Race, Ethnicity, Nation* (Harvard University Press, 2017).

bell hooks, *All About Love: New Visions* (Harper Perennial, 2000).

Reece Jones, *Violent Borders: Refugees and the Right to Move* (Verso Books, 2019).

Muthoni Likimani, *Passbook Number F.47927: Women and Mau Mau in Kenya* (Nonis Publicity, 2001).

Mahmood Mamdani, *Citizen and Subject: Contemporary Africa and the Legacy of Late Colonialism* (Princeton University Press, 1996).

Toni Morrison, *Playing in the Dark: Whiteness and the Literary Imagination* (Harvard University Press, 1992).

FURTHER READING

Toni Morrison, *The Origin of Others* (Harvard University Press, 2017).

Michael Nest, *Coltan* (Polity Press, 2011).

George Orwell, *Homage to Catalonia* (Penguin Classics, 2000).

George Orwell, *Why I Write* (essay) (Penguin, 2004).

Bertrand Russell, *In Praise of Idleness* (Routledge, 2004).

Edward W. Said, *Orientalism* (Penguin, 2003).

Edward W. Said, *Reflections on Exile and Other Essays* (Harvard University Press, 2002).

Ngũgĩ wa Thiong'o, *Decolonising the Mind: The Politics of Language in African Literature* (James Currey, 2009).

Luise White, *The Comforts of Home: Prostitution in Colonial Nairobi* (University of Chicago Press, 1990).

And anything by Bessie Head.